— ON A —
# *Wisconsin*
## FAMILY FARM

# ON A
# *Wisconsin*
# FAMILY FARM

*Historic Tales of Character, Community and Culture*

*May the stories in this book inspire you to share your stories with the loved ones in your life.*

*Corey A. Geiger*

COREY A. GEIGER

THE
History
PRESS

Published by The History Press
Charleston, SC
www.historypress.com

First published 2021

Manufactured in the United States

ISBN 9781467145282

Library of Congress Control Number: 2020948646

*Notice*: The information in this book is true and complete to the best of our knowledge. It is offered without guarantee on the part of the author or The History Press. The author and The History Press disclaim all liability in connection with the use of this book.

*To America's farm women, especially Anna Burich, Julia Pritzl and Rosalie Geiger; my farm girl sister, Angela; and my farm girl wife, Krista. In memory of my faithful farming father, Randy. His earthly life ended while writing this book, and he now belongs to heaven.*

# PRAISE FOR HOMESTEADER'S HOPE

This book was developed from the Homesteaders' Hope column that appeared in *The Brillion News*, a weekly newspaper based in Brillion, Wisconsin. The following comments came directly from fans of the column and the content found in this book.

*When Corey approached me with the idea to have the Homesteaders' Hope column in* The Brillion News, *I thought it sounded like a good addition to the newspaper. It turned out to be a great addition. Corey's column has become a staple of our paper that people look forward to reading, and it even attracted new eyes to the paper.*

*The magic of Corey's writing is that while it educates people on previous eras, you don't have to know the history and characters to become enthralled in his writing. Corey's passion, effort, and research that he puts into the column is unparalleled and jumps off the page, leaving readers ready for the next installment.*

*—David Nordby, editor,* The Brillion News

*A friend gave me a copy of* The Brillion News, *which included Homesteaders' Hope. I was most impressed with your article. You wove a wonderful narrative around, what had to be, well-researched genealogical information. My guess is you were able to enrich the factual data with family tales, history, and "legend," much of which was probably* oral history. You created very readable documentary evidence for future generations. For this you have my thanks and admiration.

What you have compiled is not just important for your family and your locality but for all of us to appreciate the struggles, efforts, and challenges that brought prosperity to the generations that have preceded us. Few people seem to be interested in that perspective today, and it is so important to help future generations find their direction. As Marcus Tullius Cicero wrote, "Not to know what happened before you were born is to remain forever a child." And, adult perspective is often sadly lacking in our world today.

Again, thanks so much for your article. You give me much hope and have enriched my day.

—*Michael Glandt, Wisconsin*

How nice it was to read about the old time polka bands. Being up in age…I knew them all and it was just great to read your "old time" story. Thanks for it…let's hope you do more.

—*Lois Hansen Linzmaier, Georgia*

Let me congratulate you on your great articles in The Brillion News! I wait every week to see and read the next issue. Keep up the good job!

—*Gary Wallander, Wisconsin*

Every week I look forward to the Homesteaders' Hope that appears in The Brillion News. I am thoroughly enjoying the historical background of the area.

—*Margaret Miller Watson, Illinois*

I'm enjoying your weekly Homesteaders' Hope column in The Brillion News and actually look forward to it! It's a great diversion to take a step back in time!

It's a great history lesson too, so keep up the good work—I hope you'll write a book someday, too!

—*Lynn T., Wisconsin*

Just a note to tell you that I really enjoy your Homesteaders' Hope articles. You do an excellent job; I hope it's not coming to an end too soon. You've obviously spent a lot of time and work on it. Thank you for your good work.

—*Jim Voss, Virginia*

*I just finished your published article, "The Race for a Vaccine." It is well-written, so informative, and a very appropriate message for our present situation. I learned some valuable information. So much of your article reminds us of how vulnerable our earth and its inhabitants are at any time. Thank you again for your research and excellent article....I look forward to reading more.*

*—Beverly Loofboro, Wisconsin*

*Your last article—"Red John or Black John?"—was hilarious!!! It would be worth ordering* The Brillion News *if only it had your most interesting articles.*

*—Joanne Ebert, Wisconsin*

*I realize that I've written once or twice in the past, but I can't help but write just one more time. Each week your Homesteaders' Hope articles are the highlight of my week.*

*I so enjoy hearing about the "olden golden" years, when the immigrants came to our country, and all the things they did to survive. Actually when you shared the experiences on your trip to China, I had to giggle in how you explained the chicken legs, fish eggs, duck tongue, and fried tendons. Hilarious!!!*

*Just so you know that I also ate many of those forms of meat, with the exception of a donkey burger. Yikes!!!*

*My father was the main guy in our neighborhood butchering days. I can still see him with his shirt sleeves rolled up and mixing that summer sausage in a huge wash tube. Yep—I enjoyed liver, heart, tongue, gizzards, and pig brains.*

*Now when my two sons butcher and I ask them to save those parts of the animal for their mother, they have a rather pale look on their face. Ha!*

*I have an idea (as if you haven't thought about it): How about putting all of those articles in a book?*

*I would be the first one to purchase it, no matter the price.*

*—Joanne Ebert, Wisconsin*

*I really enjoyed reviewing your book. I found it very interesting and readable.*

*It really is an excellent look at immigrant (pioneer) life in the Upper Midwest. It's a great perspective on early agriculture, economic development, and religion's role among immigrants, among many other things.*

It really underscores the value and importance of recording family history and saving old correspondence.

Some of the anecdotes are particularly intriguing. For example, the need for name changes. I especially enjoyed the discussion of the lime kilns. I'm part of a group that hikes Ice Age trails and others in the Southern Kettle Moraine a couple of times a week. Occasionally, our hikes take us by what's called the "Pioneer Lime Kiln," which always leads to some discussion about lime's role back in those days.

All in all, a job well done.

—*Steven Larson, Wisconsin*

# CONTENTS

# PREFACE

To be candid, I grew up with this book…it just wasn't written yet. An ambitious farmer, my grandfather Norbert Geiger Sr. had purchased three additional dairy farms by 1966 as a fourth-generation dairyman. Norbert was long on labor with seven living sons and five equally hardworking daughters. Norman Rockwell would have declared the farm was near picture-perfect Americana.

Everything changed in a flash on August 6, 1966, when Norbert suffered a massive heart attack. He instantly died and left behind a dozen children ages one to eighteen. His widow, Monica, stepped up as the farm manager and held together her brood of twelve children who were all assigned farm or household responsibilities. They clung to one another as if on a ship during a most tumultuous sea voyage. On a trajectory to become a Catholic priest, my then-sixteen-year-old father, Randy, ear tag number five in birth order, left the seminary and began his new vocation of dairy farmer.

With a high school diploma in hand, Randy began with a rent-to-own option on one of Monica Geiger's dairy farms as a way to get his start in life but also to reduce the workload for his siblings and mother. My parents, Randy and Rosalie, married in 1969, and I happened upon the scene in 1972.

As the years ticked by, "Corey the Kid"—as my Geiger aunts Martha, Monica and MaryAnn called me—was always in the background. As a tagalong during busy days on the farm, I largely entertained myself and turned my hearing radar up during adult conversations between my parents,

Grandma Geiger, aunts and uncles, who were constantly moving in every direction. Not many punches were held back during those candid farming conversations. Work had to be done, and the language was blunt.

Like a sponge, I simply soaked it all in.

Then, in 1981, my parents made a business pivot.

My maternal grandparents, Elmer and Julia Pritzl, were overworked on their 215-acre dairy farm, which they had operated for forty-two years. This fatigue came at a time when their daughter Rosalie and son-in-law Randy were looking for a bigger spread. In rather short order, my parents put together a plan to sell their farm to Randy's brother Albert Geiger (ear tag eleven in birth order), who had recently graduated high school. That sale allowed my parents to purchase Elmer and Julia Pritzl's Whispering Pines Estate. The farm's family footprint dated back to 1867, and Rosalie would be the fifth generation to till its soil and nurture its animals.

As they were strapped for labor, I immediately began doing work meant for a teenage boy. Starting at age ten, I was chopping silage, baling hay and milking cows. I was part of it all. The adult conversations continued, and Corey the Kid kept right on listening and taking it in. Hardly a week went by that didn't include Grandpa and Grandma Pritzl stopping by to work or make a social call on our farm. Some of those weeks would include two, three or four trips into the homestead house built by John and Anna Burich, Grandma Julia's parents.

The stories rolled off their tongues and were kept locked away for safekeeping into my photographic mind. Grandma Julia had a bumper crop of stories, as she had been born and raised in the homestead house. Like me, Julia grew up hearing all the adult conversations as a youth in the background of countless adult conversations. Her ears were receiving sound waves that reached deep into Wisconsin's massive influx of immigrants. Elmer more than held his own telling those narratives at the kitchen table, as his mother-in-law, Anna Burich, lived with the couple the final fifteen years of her life.

Farming and fun became synonymous in my teenage years. Saturday's winter firewood–making campaigns always came with two or three work breaks chock full of vintage stories from Grandpa Elmer. A quick-witted fellow, no story was ever the same. Work and fun had become one.

In my teenage years, my parents implored me go out for the county dairy cattle judging team, an activity that teaches youth how to select the best cows for future dairy farm profitability. Junior judges simply had to line up cows from first to fourth. The senior-level team members had to give two minutes of oral reasons as if a lawyer in a courtroom making their case to a jury. Each set of reasons was worth fifty points with an automatic ten-point deduction for looking at your notes. The facts mattered, the proper rank of the points was paramount and being articulate sold the story. These traits later would serve me well in my life's chosen vocation of journalist.

Initially, I got bounced from the dairy cattle judging team, as my kid sister, Angela, who was five years younger, beat me out for the last spot.

Mom insisted I try out again. I didn't make it on the second try, either. A third try was inevitable, as Mom stopped a sentence short of issuing an ultimatum—but her eyes told me to go.

That's when my dairy cattle judging coach Bill Borgwardt instilled a new approach to make the county's dairy judging team. The conversation went like this:

"You are smart."

"You know cows."

"You can tell stories."

"Just place the cows, drop the clipboard and tell us a story," continued the steady influence. It meant everything to me.

With that, I dropped the clipboard—my security blanket, if you will—and took the next step in my skill's development. I've been telling stories ever since.

When I was a college student at the University of Wisconsin–Madison, Dr. David Dickson was the legendary dairy cattle judging coach. Dickson's Badger dairy cattle judging teams won twice as many oral reasons titles as any other team at the Intercollegiate Dairy Cattle Judging Contest. That national contest would be the equivalent of the NCAA Championship of dairy cattle judging. In coaching me, Dr. Dickson spent more time developing my understanding of the English language than he did teaching the nuances of dairy cattle judging. He had a way of pulling out the best in an individual.

Knowing that there was an opening on the *Hoard's Dairyman* editorial team, Dickson recommended me for the associate editor position after editor W.D. Knox called him looking for leads. Bill, as I later called him, was a towering figure in the dairy industry, serving as the third lead editor of the publication dating back to 1885. Dickson made this recommendation knowing I only had one journalism course to my credit and that my university diploma would not be conferred for another fourteen months.

A week after that phone call between Dickson and Knox, I traveled to Fort Atkinson to have a conversation—at least that was my thought—with W.D. "Bill" Knox, E.C. "Gene" Meyer, E.H. "Ewing" Row and S.A. "Steve" Larson. Eventually, these men would tally a combined two hundred years of editorial service to the publication. While I thought the afternoon gathering was a get-to-know-one-another session, those four men had other ideas. After four hours of dialogue and two writing tests, Knox huddled with his cohorts and then offered me a position as associate editor that very afternoon.

After a week's contemplation, I accepted his offer and started the following June and eventually graduated from college in December 1995. Once again, I was Corey the Kid as Bill, Gene, Ewing and Steve collectively molded me into a communication guru and a world traveler. Not bad for a kid who never scurried more than thirty miles outside of Wisconsin until his senior year in high school.

Once at *Hoard's Dairyman*, I embraced the collaborative environment where everyone read everyone's copy—veteran or rookie—and offered input. All comments were considered by the editor routing the copy. As the months and years turned on the calendar, my copy received fewer red marks from the editors. Marlene Brunner, who would amass fifty-eight years as the publication's chief grammar authority, eventually bought fewer red pencils.

The more I traveled for *Hoard's Dairyman*, the more I also grew to appreciate the talents of those who mentored me. Unlike the curious cow that is constantly reaching over the fence for what's perceived to be better grass, farm boy Corey had confirmed that the grass was greener on my side of the fence.

As my grandparents settled into their eighties, I knew it was time to capture oral histories and ask the questions of their stories for which I could not connect the dots. At first, I hid recorders under tablecloths, knowing the conservative couple would clam up if they knew my motives. My ever-shrewd grandparents eventually caught wind of my plan, and one day Grandpa Elmer took the recorder out from under the tablecloth and set it on the table. He kept talking and so did Grandma Julia, who shared that the notes and photos under her bed would be mine, but only after her death.

At her passing in 2011, while sorting and cleaning their home, I found a treasure trove. However, like a jigsaw puzzle with pieces scattered everywhere, I first had to put the story together.

Here's that story.

# Acknowledgements

Everyone needs an advocate.

For many of us, our parents were our first unabashed supporters. Such was the case with my parents, Randy and Rosalie Geiger, who encouraged me in my endeavors. They gave me the opportunity to blaze my own trail, and they were there to lift me up when I fell short of my goals. Most importantly, my parents provided me the space for trial and error, allowed me to make mistakes and let me learn from those events. That isn't always the case in today's world, where some parents want to bubble-proof their children's world. However, full-time farm parents don't have time to fly in the helicopter and save the day for their children. So, my pants got dusted off often after I stood up from my falls.

As the 150th anniversary for our family dairy farm approached, I could not coax my parents into throwing a bash to celebrate the six generations of family farming. To be candid, they were getting tired after forty-eight years of milking cows every day and cropping the land with all its annual work cycles. After a number of jousts, I dropped the idea.

That's when I came up with a new way to hold my own weekly party by starting the Homesteaders' Hope series in my hometown paper, *The Brillion News*. After pitching the idea to editor David Nordby and the fourth-generation owners Elizabeth Wenzel, Darcy Zander-Feinauer and Kris Bastian, they all agreed that I should write a few sample columns. After they read them, a green light was given to forge ahead.

The opening column, which appeared both in print and online, took off like gangbusters. That's when we collectively decided to pull the columns back to print only. I asked for no compensation with the caveat that I could also retain the copyright. As the column continued, Raymond Selner opened an entirely new narrative by translating all the historic Satorie family letters that had been written in the Czech language.

Everyone needs a cheerleader. For this book, my wife, Krista, was captain of the squad. While I initially had the idea of self-publishing a book one day, she was convinced that I was not dreaming big enough. That's when she began researching publishers and helped develop a marketing plan.

A number of publishers quickly expressed interest, but one stood out above the crowd—Arcadia Publishing. After our first conversation with John Rodrigue, we instantly had a connection. We hashed out the details and completed a publishing contract.

As that took place, I took a recess from writing my Homesteaders' Hope column after sixty-six renditions. That's because six-plus years of planning were about to come to a crescendo as my wife and I were co-chairs for the 134th National Holstein Convention that welcomed over 1,200 dairy cattle breeders from thirty-eight states and nineteen countries to Appleton, Wisconsin. At that same June 2019 convention, I was elected the sixty-fifth president of Holstein Association USA, founded in 1885. Two weeks later, a trip to China ensued, where I gave five presentations and interacted with the Chinese team who runs *Hoard's Dairyman China*. That publication had been launched two years earlier, and I was in the middle of it all.

As these events were unfolding, my parents took it upon themselves to plan their own 50th wedding anniversary party and 152nd celebration for the farm. Relatives from far and wide came on that August 3 day. It was a celebration of a lifetime; we honored a marriage of 50 years, and the family's historic archives were flung wide open. That proved to be a gathering many would remember for reasons unknown to anyone that day.

Just two weeks later, my father was flipping hay in a process called side raking. It's the last step before baling dry hay. He was working in the very field that serves as the epicenter for this book.

The trouble that day was that he felt terrible—so terrible that Mom drove him straight to the hospital, where Appleton doctors placed him on a Flight for Life helicopter ride to Milwaukee's Aurora St. Luke's Medical Center. There his farm siblings each got to have a conversation with him. As my father's eighteen-day saga in the cardiovascular intensive care unit labored on, his heart surgeon, Dr. Will Fischer, told me that my plate was overflowing with responsibilities and that it was humanly impossible to keep up my pace. He suggested that I offload or postpone some projects.

Days later, my dad died. Complications from his heart attack would not allow his heart to sustain life. My writing moxie rolled downhill into a ditch like raging waters from a springtime flood.

As I grieved, others began lifting me up. It took a lot of effort, but their collective action breathed energy into my soul.

"When are you going to write again?"

"Those stories were great. It would be great to hear more."

"Your narratives have caused us to share our family's history with one another."

The emails, calls and notes flowed in like calm water traversing a brook.

That's when I reached out to John Rodrigue and shared my situation. He gave me heaps of understanding and plenty of space.

Finally, I suggested a new book deadline knowing that the creative cat in me could not meet the original December 20, 2019 deadline. After some thought, I suggested August 2020—that would be one year following my father's passing—by then, this book could be "the best of me."

In March, the final journey began.

To help me cross the finish line, *Hoard's Dairyman* art director C. Todd Garrett headed up photo scanning and repair on the historic images found within.

My mom, Rosalie Geiger; wife, Krista Knigge; aunt and uncle Annie and Bob Krueger; sister Angela Zwald; uncle Albert Geiger; and father-in-law, Pete Knigge, stepped up their reviews.

Uncle Albert, the Kocourek and Krepline families and a host of others answered my calls and texts to help with farm work. Yes, with my father's death, I became co-manager of the family farm now pushing four hundred acres. To the firewood brigade headed up by Greg Schuh, Kenny Wilhelm and a host of deer hunting and farming friends, you proved vital in keeping the historic homestead house heated this winter.

In an effort to make the narrative even better, I asked my former supervisor, mentor and retired managing editor of *Hoard's Dairyman*, Steve Larson, to review the manuscript as well. Steve and I co-edited *We Need a Show*, the fiftieth anniversary book on the world's greatest dairy show—World Dairy Expo. Steve's final edits were so valuable.

Then, with copy and photos ready, final book creation was turned over to John Rodrigue and his teammates at Arcadia Publishing/The History Press.

# INTRODUCTION

Have you ever pondered why so many people with Bohemian and German heritage settled in Northeast Wisconsin?

To understand the answer to that question, we must rewind our clocks nearly 150 years. Wisconsin had just celebrated its 20th year as a state. Page scrolls through the 1868 plat books reveal that many forty-acre parcels were still for sale, as loggers hadn't even harvested trees in some instances.

That was all about to change.

And quickly.

Central to this work is 150 years of continuous family ownership in the Burich, Pritzl and now Geiger families. In the three most recent generations, the farm was passed through daughters Anna Burich, Julia Pritzl and Rosalie Geiger, not sons, as was customary. It creates a unique narrative of female ownership in an era that started 14 years before Congress ratified the Nineteenth Amendment to the Constitution giving women the right to vote.

As this 150-year journey unfolds, you will meet a cast of characters who have long since passed from this world. Along the way, stories of neighbors are woven into the narrative. These were the folks who interacted with one another to build America's Dairyland by working together to construct farmsteads, loan money and create a social support network—mostly without government support.

A maternal maverick, Julia's mother, born Anna Satorie, went against cultural norms and became the owner of her family's homestead in 1905. That is when her father, Wencel Satorie, asked that the name of Anna Satorie, a single lady, be recorded on the land deed.

In exchange, Anna cared for her widowed father until his dying day on November 1, 1920. It was a fifteen-year payback.

While the legal title on the forty-acre parcel was never updated to indicate that Anna had married, abstractors noted the owner as "Mrs. John A. Burich" in subsequent county plat books because local community and its culture weren't quite ready for the moniker "Mrs. Anna Burich" or the even bolder "Anna Burich."

Wencel died during the Sunday morning church service two days after Julia's second birthday. This short line connection to an actual immigrant—Wencel, through his daughter Anna, and then to granddaughter Julia—helped preserve a treasure trove of historical documents and colorful stories. Photos backed up the historic record she kept for future generations, and Julia labeled them all.

As for Anna, she was among the toughest pioneer women.

By age sixty-two, she had earned the title of unquestioned farm leader and family matriarch. Up until this point, she had been an equal to her husband, John, who routinely consulted with her on all business matters.

In 1939, John Burich died, and Anna alone carried the family flag.

She was more than ready.

By 1939, every male in her immediate family had died—two infant sons, her father, her father-in-law, three of her husband's brothers and finally her husband. The burden also included losing her sister-in-law, Lizzie, who was her maid of honor, to tuberculosis and burying her thirteen-year-old daughter, who died of polio. Anna stood alone and faced many decisions, as her remaining four adult daughters had married.

After reflecting on her situation, she reopened the farm's business plan. Like the famed Bible story, Anna chose a young David in her life to rebuild the economic health of her family's once thriving farm, which had become fatigued by the economic pounding of the Dirty Thirties and the Great Depression. Anna chose her youngest daughter, Julia, and her unproven city-boy husband, Elmer, who had been married less than a year. That decision proved pivotal, even as neighbors initially may have thought that Anna had lost her mind.

In her lifetime, Anna Burich was never formally recognized as a community leader. However, Anna, her daughter Julia and other women like them are the bedrock on which thriving communities develop.

Anna, Julia and the many women like them provided the hope to fuel the family's dreams.

The hope that ultimately built the family homestead.

The hope that provided the inspiration for *On a Wisconsin Family Farm*.

# 1

# The Trail Less Traveled

The family farm is a living, breathing entity.

For those who never had the opportunity to grow up on a family farm, that statement is almost beyond comprehension. However, for those who were blessed with the opportunity, they know that the family farm has a pulse. We live on her land, till her fields, gather her crops and take care of her animals in order to survive and even thrive as a family.

That's the life pulse in which I was nurtured and developed.

Our six-generation family farm talked to me for decades in her own voice. She gradually revealed generations of long-kept secrets to me. I simply had to use all my senses—sight, hearing, smell, taste and touch—to reap the stories. Each sense delivered a unique narrative with its own attributes.

In the spring and early summer of 2006, our family farm kept whispering deep into my soul. By June, Robert Frost's famed poem from 1916, "The Road Not Taken," was constantly replaying in my mind like a song ringing from the radio airwaves. The poem speaks of two roads that diverge in the woods. Frost laments that he could not travel both trails.

Both roads were fair. One was well traveled, and the other needed wear.

That's where I stood as the roads diverged: one trail was cut deep into the forest in the summer of 1906, the other during the spring of 2006 by yours truly using a chainsaw, logging chains and a tractor.

On a hot sunny day on July 2, 2006, with leaves scattered like a blanket on the forest floor from a heavy hailstorm the night before, I borrowed that poem to create a series of nineteen signs. Those signs, mounted on posts

The sixth-generation family farm was the setting for a wedding proposal by Corey Geiger to Krista Knigge. Later, the couple's parents, Pete and Theo Knigge and Rosalie and Randy Geiger, joined to celebrate. *Author's collection.*

staked into the ground, breathed life into a lengthy proposal for my soon-to-be bride, Krista. The narrative strung out through a forty-acre parcel described our life together up until that moment and detailed the grassy trail that needed wear.

With signs in place, my father, Randy, received a call indicating the plan was ready to be set in motion. From the farmhouse kitchen where our family had gathered for generations, he asked Krista to go for a ride in the farm pickup.

She agreed.

As they neared the trail late that Sunday morning, he slowed to a stop and dropped her off at the entrance of the woods. Before departing, he handed her a handwritten note with instructions. The farm truck and its mostly missing muffler barked out his departure.

The next phase of the plan was in motion.

Krista read the note and began walking, jogging and then running along the grassy trail as she quickly surmised that her beau was about to ask for her hand in marriage. The woods swirled with fragrances wafting from the broken leaves ripped open by the hail that had fallen from the sky the night before.

The family farm was opening up its airwaves once again.

At the end of that road—after the nineteenth sign—I knelt on one knee waiting to ask for her hand in marriage.

For me it felt like an eternity of a wait.

As it turns out, Krista could not read or run fast enough.

"Yes!" she exclaimed before I could even ask the question.

One hour later, our parents walked the same trail and joined us for a picnic.

## One Story Separated by One Hundred Years

I'd like to think I came up with that romantic idea all on my own. However, the inspiration came from a story that was one hundred years old that very year.

On June 12, 1906, two twenty-eight-year-olds—Anna Satorie and John Burich—joined their lives in front of God, their family and friends through Holy Matrimony at St. Mary's Catholic Church in Reedsville, Wisconsin. By the standards of the day, the couple was a bit old. However, an instigator named Lizzie Burich convinced the man and woman that they were right for each other—to make a life together. She was the maid of honor that day and had definitely earned the privilege.

Anna and John had cut their own trail that year to connect their family farms. In 2006, it had stood for a century as the trail more traveled.

Was the marriage of Anna and John a business proposition, love or a little of both?

## Two Mothers Passed

Anna Satorie, the bride on that day, was born on July 6, 1877.

Just one year prior to Anna's birth, her parents, Wencel and Anna Satorie, took out a mortgage to buy a forty-acre parcel at the end of today's Jerabek Lane on a section of land known as the "The Rock" to locals. It lies a short jaunt west of Reedsville, Wisconsin.

Matchmaker Elizabeth "Lizzie" Burich successfully orchestrated the marriage of her best friend Anna Satorie and brother John J. Burich on June 12, 1906. *Author's collection.*

There, the Satorie family carved out a new life in America.

Wencel and Anna had three children: Caroline, Mary and Anna. Wencel's mother, Mary, also lived with the family, having made the voyage from her native Bohemia, now a part of the modern-day Czech Republic.

In her early days, young Anna was known as "Annie" to her immediate family, as her mother bore the same name. Caroline, the oldest, died as a young teenager. Mary, who was six years older than Anna, married Joseph Tikalsky in 1891. The middle daughter was named after Wencel's mother.

That left the deeply loyal Anna.

As the last sibling at home for well over a decade, she stayed in the log cabin to take care of her ailing mother and help her healthy father with the farm work. Anna was a strong young lady who wore a men's size nine shoe and stood nearly as tall as all the Bohemian men in the neighborhood.

The years ticked by until Anna's mother died on April 27, 1905, at age fifty-six.

Anna, now twenty-seven, was still living at home with her sixty-five-year-old father, Wencel. She was quickly on her way to becoming an old maid, as the average American woman married at age twenty-one, according to U.S. Census Bureau data. Two friends of John and Anna—Antonia Burich and Anton Novak—would eventually fall into that category by becoming an old maid and a confirmed bachelor, respectively.

That's when another life force entered into the equation.

Anna was friends with the exuberant and by all accounts strikingly stunning Alzbeta Burich. Known to her English-speaking friends as Elizabeth, she was called Lizzie by her closest friends. Born on January 24, 1885, Lizzie was everything that Anna was not: she was pretty, exceedingly confident and, by all accounts, the life of the party. Anna and Lizzie often paired up together at church events.

Anna was the steady and stable friend.

Lizzie was the instigator.

Lizzie was also a matchmaker.

She convinced Anna to come along with her to the local dance halls. A favorite for the area's Bohemians was Kubale's Dance Hall just two miles from the farm. Lizzie thought Anna would be a perfect catch for her older brother John. However, Lizzie had to convince John of that notion.

Like Anna, John was dutifully loyal. Born on April 20, 1878, John worked like a mule sunup to sundown. The Burich family had amassed 215 acres of farmland, worked by horses, and also milked twenty-four cows by hand.

And like Anna, John lost his mother about the same time.

John and Anna's bridal party included (*left to right, seated*) Elizabeth Burich Kirch, Anna and John Burich and Frank Burich; (*standing*) Antonia Burich, Anton Novak, Barbara Burich Shimek, Tom Burich, Mary Turensky Gartke and Mike Vechart. *Author's collection.*

Josephina Burich, John's mother, came down with stomach problems in early 1904. After a number of visits to area doctors, John's father, Albert, took Josephina by train to a specialist in Chicago, Illinois, as the family had relatives in the Windy City. After examination, the physician determined Josephina had stomach cancer. With no treatment options, Albert and Josephina returned to Reedsville, where Josephina died on September 3, 1904.

That left the sixty-seven-year-old Albert and his industrious son John with a lot of work.

John did have five other siblings. Older sister Anna Shimek had married Emil and started their life together. Meanwhile, brother Frank had a well drilling business, brother Thomas was not cut out for life on the farm and eventually made his way to Chicago and brother Louis did not have full control of his mental faculties. And then, of course, there was Lizzie.

## MEET AT THE DANCE HALL

Lizzie had her work cut out for her.

Anna had self-esteem issues. So concerned with her looks, Anna posed for only one set of formal pictures in her life—on her wedding day. She would not even stand with her adult daughters years later at a photography studio for a family photo. That was after her loving daughters spent hours primping her.

Anna was a rough, tough pioneer woman who could work as hard as any man. The few candid photos of Anna almost always show her with arms folded and a look on her face as if a pending battle was about to break out. A battle to break the camera and get back to work.

Even though she was concerned about her looks, Anna was smart as they came by local standards, with an eighth-grade education. She was an excellent bookkeeper and kept solid finance ledgers, just as her father, Wencel, had done for his family farm. She could read and write both Bohemian and English. She could hold her own speaking German, too.

While John was a dashing fellow, he could not read. Strapped for labor, Albert and Josephina had pulled John out of St. Mary's School when he was in the second grade. He wasn't the only boy pulled from school in those days, as farm work trumped an education because families had to put food on the table.

Illiterate John lacked the confidence to ask Anna out on a date. Had he stayed in school, he would have known Anna far better because the two had started out in the same grade.

Lizzie worked her magic.

After that first dance and a nudge from Lizzie, John and Anna began courting.

In short order, John and Anna took—or shall we say created—the trail less traveled as referred to in Frost's poem, passing routinely on the corners of each other's homesteads. And as the spark of the relationship firmly took hold, a trail was formally created, connecting Wencel Satorie's farm to that of Albert Burich's homestead.

## TWO FATHERS OFFER APPROVAL

Knowing that they might need to further nudge the relationship along, the fathers got involved, too. Each widower sold his farm to his children.

On July 25, 1905, Albert Burich (*center*) sold his farm to his son John A. Burich (*left*). Elizabeth "Lizzie" Burich signed as a legal witness. *Author's collection.*

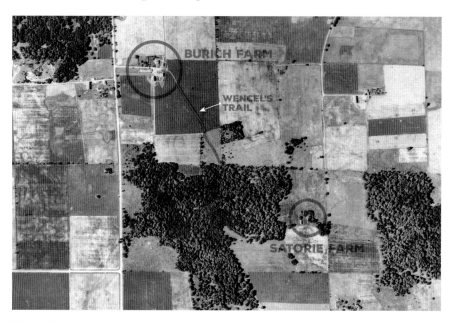

The trail between the Satorie and Burich homesteads became so important that USDA photographers could see it via aerial images in 1938. *USDA and the Arthur Robinson Map Library at the University of Wisconsin–Madison.*

On July 11, 1905, Wencel Satorie sold to "Annie Satorie, my daughter, all the balance of real estate and personal property that I will have accumulated by the time of my death," for one dollar. With Wencel's signature, his precious Annie became the first woman to buy and own land in the Rockland Township.

Things had started cooking at the Burich farm, too.

Just two weeks later, on July 24, 1905, Lizzie Burich inked her name with a bold fountain pen stroke as witness as to her father, Albert, selling the farm to brother John. Of course, John had quitclaim deeds in which he would pay an inheritance to each of his siblings for a number of years to come. However, John had acquired the entire Burich family homestead.

From all reports, Lizzie had an audacious smile on her face as she signed that bill of sale dated July 24, 1905. She had pulled it off!

John would marry Anna the next year.

Now that family business was done, the twenty-one-year-old Lizzie needed to find a splendid maid of honor dress.

But for John and Anna, not only would they marry and buy their respective family farms, but they also agreed to care for their fathers for life That commitment included caring for John's mentally challenged brother Louis. John and Anna would care for Louis in perpetuity, or what lawyers in the pioneer days would call "for the rest of his natural life."

Even so, John and Anna took the path less traveled by in those days and created a new road in their life journey together. That road is both literal and real.

That's because Anna's father, Wencel, would continue to carve that road from his log cabin to his daughter's new home over the next fourteen years as he wintered with John and Anna each year and then returned to his log cabin in spring. To this very day, the trail travels between the Burich family homestead to "Grandma's 40." That Grandma was Anna Satorie, who went on to become Grandma Anna Burich.

# 2

# THIS MARRIAGE CAME
# WITH FOUR MEN

After nearly twenty-nine years as a single woman, Anna Satorie wed John Burich on June 12, 1906. While most new brides today would leave their parents and move into their husbands' homes, there was far more involved in the situation for the nuptial-blessed Mrs. John A. Burich.

While it's true that Anna moved into the homestead home of her husband, John, this wedding-day move came with three more men: Albert, Wencel and Louis. That's because most pioneer farm families took care of their own. Back in those days there was no Social Security, no Medicare, and retirement homes and assisted living had yet to enter America's lexicon.

Family was your bedrock.

Family was your lifeline.

## ANNA'S NEW HOUSEMATES

John's father, Albert Burich, a sixty-seven-year-old widower, was still living in the slightly updated pioneer home featuring a mix of log cabin and clapboard siding. Albert, known in the family's Bohemian-speaking household as Vojtech, and his parents, Thomas and Mary Burich, had constructed the patchwork house thirty-nine years earlier.

Then there was Anna's beloved father, Wencel, also a widower. Wencel, known as Václav to his Czech-speaking friends, would live with Anna and John from late fall to early spring.

Wencel Satorie built this log cabin for his family. After his wife's passing, he would live in this cabin from April to November and overwinter with his daughter Anna and her husband, John. *Author's collection.*

Around April, he would take his horse and oxen team back to his log cabin on the Rock and start planting tobacco, wheat and a substantial vegetable crop. When snow began to fly, he would return like a modern-day snowbird to Anna and John's slightly more insulated home, which featured far better cooking from his daughter Anna.

If that wasn't enough, Louis Burich also lived with the couple.

Known as Alois in the family's native Bohemian tongue, Louis was John's younger brother by three years. As Louis was unable to completely care for himself, John had agreed to provide for him as part of the farm purchase.

So, there it was, Anna and four grown men all living in her "new" home. That was a lot of cooking that came with the June 12, 1906 wedding-day bliss.

So much for a honeymoon period.

## OVER FOUR COMBINED DECADES

Little did Anna know that this would be a decades-long obligation—a period of twenty years. The couple's fathers, Albert and Wencel, would far outlive

33

the average early 1900s American male who lived to forty-seven years of age, according to data from the Centers for Disease Control and Prevention.

Anna's father-in-law, Albert Burich, would live another decade, passing away on September 3, 1916. He died at age seventy-nine while the family was out in the barn hand-milking their Holstein cows.

Her father, Wencel Satorie, would live fourteen more years, passing away on November 1, 1920. Unexpectedly, he had a massive stroke during a Sunday morning mass in the recently constructed St. Mary's Church. He was eighty. As a devout Catholic, Wencel could not have conjured a better way to leave this earthly world.

Brother-in-law Louis Burich died last out of the three men Anna inherited with her marriage to John. Louis lived a far shorter life than Albert and Wencel, passing away on January 13, 1926. He was forty-five, a few years short of the average life expectancy of that era.

By the time this trio died, Anna had given birth to seven children—three of whom would also die by 1926. The most tragic death would take place two days after Christmas in December 1926 when daughter Cecilia, an eighth grader, died from polio. The students of the entire eighth grade class were pallbearers.

With that tragic death—just twenty years after her marriage—Anna would bury six family members who all lived under her roof. That was life in pioneer America. There were no counseling programs. You clung to your faith, and you had to be one tough cookie.

Anna did both in spades.


## Land Eased Burden

For these promises from Anna, Wencel allowed his daughter to purchase his homestead farm, a forty-acre parcel, for $1. Meanwhile, she had to promise to pay her only living sister, Mary Tikalsky, wife of Joseph Tikalsky, $300 upon their father's death.

Anna's husband, John, had to fork over far more cash.

For his 160-acre purchase, the twenty-eight-year-old John Burich signed a much lengthier agreement for the Burich farm detailed in the abstract of title filed at the Manitowoc County Courthouse. The full abstract of title consists of 116 legal entries over 43 pages. Every loan, property lien and land transfer is legally recorded on it.

In purchasing the family homestead for $1, Anna also signed a note indicating she would give her only living sister, Mary, and husband Joseph Tikalsky $300 at Wencel's death. *Author's collection.*

What follows is word for word from a signed agreement between John A. Burich (son) and Albert K. Burich (father) dated and signed July 24, 1905. That agreement was signed just one year before John's wedding to Anna.

*John A. Burich to Albert K. Burich for a $4,000 consideration also has agreed to:*

*1. To pay or cause to be paid to Lizzie Burich* [sister] *$400, without interest, and deliver to her one cow on demand.*

*2. To Annie Burich* [sister], *wife of Emanuel Shimek* [spelled Schimek on grave] *the sum of $50, without interest.* [Presumably, Annie received a dowry on her wedding day.]

*3. To Thomas Burich* [brother] *$350 at the time he should attain the age of 21 years, without interest.*

*4. To Louis Burich* [brother] *the sum of $350 at any time he shall vacate the premises, but so long as he shall agree to stay at home, to support, clothe and care for, furnish medical aid in case of sickness to and for said Louis Burich.*

*5. To his father, said Albert K. Burich,*

*a. The sum of $200 on demand from time to time as he may choose.*

*b. To pay or cause to be paid all just lawful debts contracted by said Albert K. Burich up to present date.*

*c. Further, said John A. Burich shall deliver to said Albert K. Burich annually during the natural life of said Albert K. Burich, one fourth of all proceeds of the farm above described such as grain, hay, potatoes, fruit, vegetables, together with one quarter (¼) of moneys received for milk, butter, and eggs, free and clear of all expenses, along with 200 pounds of fresh pork.*

*d. Said Albert K. Burich to have use of rooms in house.*

*e. Should Albert K. Burich, for any reasonable cause be unable to live in the same house as said John A. Burich, then in such case John A. Burich shall pay to said Albert K. Burich the just sum of $1,500, the same shall be as full payment and satisfaction of this bond.*

*f. Further agreed if said John A. Burich shall well and properly support keep, maintain, and care for said Albert K. Burich, then in such case he to pay him only one fourth of milk, moneys, each and every year, and no more.*

## A THRIFTY MAN

John quickly went to work paying off his debts.

On December 6, 1905, he paid his sister Anna Shimek $50. Thomas Burich received his $350 on April 23, 1908. Meanwhile, Lizzie Burich received $400 on November 24, 1909. Older brother Frank A. Burich was never listed in these proceedings. He presumably was well on his way to becoming a successful well driller.

Those, of course, were the easy debts.

John and Anna were on the financial hook for Albert and Louis. Ten years later, Judge John Chloupek released John from the bond with his late father, Albert Burich, on December 5, 1916, as recorded in the land abstract.

The similar bond for Louis Burich was released by E.S. Schmitz, special administrator for the deceased, on May 13, 1926. That, too, is duly recorded.

Now debt-free, John could enjoy the fruits of his hard labor.

## A DIFFERENT ERA

No one would rightly sign such an open-ended purchase agreement these days. It could be financial suicide.

However, that was the immigrant code. Take care of those who allowed you to live the American Dream. John and Anna did just that and also followed the rules of the Good Book, the Holy Bible.

As the couple did so, attorneys also recorded every major legal action. That ensured everyone also followed the Good Book.

# 3

# IT WASN'T PRETTY BACK HOME

When immigrant families set sail for America, the entire extended family often did not make the voyage. Such was the case for Wencel Satorie's relatives.

Wencel's sister Katerina and her husband stayed in Bohemia. An older brother, Joseph, and his family also stayed behind, as did an uncle bearing the last name Vančura.

There was good reason many Europeans left their life behind and took their chances in the New World. In some cases, drought and famine challenged a family's very existence. In other cases, families were fleeing wars that were breaking out through the region. As those wars raged, families on occasion lost all their earthly possessions. Yet in other instances, large families did not have enough assets to sustain life.

And so they set sail for America.

While it's not known for sure why Wencel took his young family to America, life was taking a turn for the worse where he grew up and spent his formative years.

*Dear Vencel,*

*So, for God's sake, I ask you to help me with some money...*

This plea headlined a letter dated April 21, 1900. It was sent from Caslav, a town located in the heart of the Bohemia, known today as the Czech Republic. The town is roughly one hour east of Prague.

*Left*: Mary Satorie and her brother Mr. Vančura posed for a photo in Caslav, Bohemia, just before Mary and her son Wencel Satorie's family set sail for America. *Author's collection.*

*Below*: With impeccable penmanship, Katerina Buresova wrote to her brother on April 20, 1900. Note "Viskozin" and "Norad Amerika" stand for Wisconsin and the United States of America. *Author's collection.*

The letter was sent by Katerina Buresova, born Katerina Satorie, to her brother Wencel, who now lived on a homestead farm just one mile west of Reedsville. That letter made it from Bohemia to Wencel's hands with a mailing address of "Viskozin" (Wisconsin) in "Norad Amerika" (North America). The envelope and letters display impeccable penmanship.

Of course, "Vencel" was Katerina's brother Wencel. For Bohemians of the era, *V* denoted the letter *W*, as the Czech language did not have the alphabetical character.

This letter penned by the desperate Katerina is one of many letters that the Satorie and Burich families saved for well over a century. Despite the impeccable cursive writing, only a skilled translator can make out the meaning of those letters between family members. That's because the mix of cursive and writing in the Bohemian or Czech language challenges the best of translators.

*April 21, 1900*

*Dear Vencel,*

*So, for God's sake, I ask you to help me with some money.*

*Praised be the Lord Jesus Christ. Dear brother and sister-in-law and all your children. I am greeting you one hundred times and send kisses. I hope [to] God that I find you in good and steady health with these few lines.*

*Dear brother and sister-in-law, it is bad with me. Rysavy* [Katerina's son-in-law] *spent all my money and he is getting worse and worse. If I have some money, he takes everything he finds, he sells everything and he beats us.*

*I was happy for Kacenka* [Katerina's daughter] *that she married well; for 10 years Rysavy was good to her. Now he beats her. She couldn't stand it anymore, so she left him. Rysavy and Kacenka had to get a divorce, and I don't know where my head is.*

*Rysavy met a widow of some sort and lays with her. I don't have any money and now the two of us have to make a living ourselves.*

*I'm old, I can't work. For God's sake, I beg you have pity over me with some money. It won't hurt you after all and God will repay you and your children; he will give happiness. We will pray for you.*

*Josef* [another brother] *would help me but he himself is a beggar, his children support him. So, I ask you not to deny me this or else I will despair, that's how bad things are with me.*

*You know me, if things weren't that bad, I wouldn't write to you. I now have Kacenka to care of and she's invalid* [a divorced woman] *and I, old and unhealthy. What should I do?*

*We cannot survive here anymore; everything is expensive and high rent; one doesn't even know what to do.*

*Katerina Buresova,*
*Caslav, Bohemia*

## THREE SIBLINGS IN WISCONSIN

As far as Katerina was concerned, her brother Wencel had struck it rich in America.

Katerina had two more siblings who were pursuing the American dream. Tomas was living a mile south of Wencel as the crow flies. A sister, Annia Satorie (born 1849), married a man named Albert Burich (born 1845). Annia and Albert farmed one mile to the east of both Wencel and Tomas, making the three Satorie family members and their respective farms located in a near perfect triangle with one-mile travel distances between all three farms.

Surely those three siblings could send money to support their presumably older sister who did not flee to America.

As for Wencel, he was named after Saint Wenceslas, who was duke of Bohemia from AD 921 to 935. Wenceslas became Bohemia's first saint canonized by the Catholic Church and is the patron saint of the Czech Republic.

English hymnwriter Jason Neale later popularized Wenceslas in the 1853 Christmas carol "Good King Wenceslas." As a result, many Bohemian cemeteries have gravestones bearing the name *Václav*—Bohemian for "Wencel."

Wencel and his wife, Anna, had come to America after the first Bohemian wave of settlers to the Reedsville area. Wencel's brother Tomas "Zadroria" and his sister Annia had arrived in the first wave.

Zadroria was an early entry in Manitowoc County's landownership plat books and on 1870 U.S. census documents. English speakers often struggled interpreting immigrants' names in conversations when taking census rolls and entering land records. Zadroria wasn't close to correct.

The Americanized version of the family's last name became Satorie. The truest English-language spelling of the Old World name can be found on

Wencel's gravestone—Satorye—as it was spelled out in the 1900 letter from Katerina. He insisted upon that even though the gravestone for his wife, Anna, who died fifteen years earlier, read Satorie. Adding to the translation confusion, Tomas's gravestone reads Satorije, while his wife, Antonie (who died five years later), lies under a stone that reads Satorie.

Older brother Tomas Satorie homesteaded an eighty-acre farm located in the same Rockland Township in which his younger brother Wencel would later establish a homestead. Tomas and his wife, Antonie, had a son named Frantisek, but he died at age fourteen. That was the only recorded boy being born to the two men. With no adult sons for Tomas or Wencel, the surname Satorie faded from the area.

Arriving roughly six years after his brother Tomas, Wencel and his wife, born Anna Moravec, came to America with two daughters, Caroline and Mary. They had few possessions. Wencel also brought his sixty-year-old mother, Mary, as Wencel's father had passed away prior to the family making the voyage across the Atlantic Ocean.

Wencel, his wife, Anna, and his mother, Mary, lived with Tomas and Antonie's family for four years. Quarters were tight in that little log cabin, especially considering Wencel and Anna also had two little girls.

Those four years clearly strained the bond of brothers, because when Wencel Satorie and his family finally forged out on their own, there was little correspondence between the family members. The family matriarch, Mary, sided with son Wencel and moved to his homestead.

Wencel had pioneered a homestead farm located at the end of a half-mile road now known as Jerabek Lane. In those days, most of Wisconsin's roads did not have names. Had there been road names, Jerabek Lane likely would have been dubbed Satorie Lane.

The family matriarch, Mary Satorie, not only immigrated to America with her son Wencel Satorie but also would later live her final years in his family's log cabin. *Author's collection.*

There, the Wencel Satorie family carved out a new life in America on a section of land known as the "Rock" to generations of local Reedsville villagers and Rockland Township inhabitants. Wencel and his family were close enough to visit his brother's family but far enough to have their own life.

By all accounts, Wencel was closer to his sister Annia and her husband, Albert, as two of the couple's daughters, Barbara and

Antonia, would be bridesmaids in the wedding of their cousin Anna and her groom John Burich.

Ironically, Barbara, Antonia and John all had fathers bearing the name Albert Burich. The two men known in those days as Vojtech were not closely related to each other. John's father died in 1916, and Barbara and Antonia's father died two years later.

As they had limited means, Wencel and Anna didn't get prime land. However, Wencel was still able to eke out a living on the Rock, named for the prominent limestone outcroppings that pushed through the soil's surface. Wencel's little piece of the Rock belongs to the much grander Niagara Escarpment that runs through the entire Great Lakes Basin.

A linen weaver by trade in the old country, Wencel became a farmer in his adopted homeland by growing tobacco, barley and wheat, and he sold firewood to the lime kilns in nearby Grimms, Wisconsin.

Hand-dug cisterns preserved precious water. A hand-pump well co-owned by Frank Kubale, and later Frank and Steve Kocourek, helped provide additional water to the farm families on their adjacent forty-acre parcels.

As far as Wencel's sister Katerina in Bohemia was concerned, her brother had great wealth to buy his "Viskozin" farm in "Norad Amerika" on March 28, 1877. It was a glorious day in her mind. She was so happy for Wencel, who also dutifully took care of their dear mother, Mary.

Katerina may have been correct in her assumptions. Based on the size of the aforementioned gravestones in old St. Mary's Cemetery, Wencel and his wife, Anna, spent more money on their grave monuments than siblings Tomas and Annia. Adding to that notion is that both family farms were sold to nonrelatives immediately after their deaths. Wencel's farm has remained in the family for well over 150 years.

## LIVED TWO MORE DECADES

Many letters and small packages—along with American cash—were sent from the brother to his sister. To ensure money made it safely to Bohemia, it was often sewn into clothing. In that way, a nosy handler of the parcel would have to be far more determined to steal the cash before it arrived at its destination in Bohemia.

Money flowed even more freely to Wencel's sister after he buried his wife, Anna, on April 25, 1905. Of course, as more money flowed, more desperate pleas came back from Bohemia. Wencel kept sending money, just like many immigrant families working in America do these days for family members still living in impoverished conditions back home.

Clearly Katerina was still finding a way to make a go of it, as another lengthy letter arrived a full two decades later.

*September 21, 1921*

*Dear Brother and Family,*

*First of all, I greet you hundred times and send kisses. I am letting you know that I received the money from you on 19ᵗʰ September. I can't even write you enough about the joy I felt.*

*Dear Friends, we have it worse than in the war* [World War I]. *Everything's expensive here:*

- *1 kilogram of flour is 8 crowns* [currency]
- *100 kilograms of potatoes, 200 crowns*
- *100 kilograms of wheat, 500 crowns.*

*Who can buy this?*

*I have 141 crowns a month....I need to live on this, clothe myself, pay rent and fuel. So imagine my poverty, dear friends.*

*Josef is dead and his wife died on August 19 at 96 years old. I now don't have anyone here; I'm abandoned. I also have to write to you that we haven't had rain since May, that is all summer! We have it tough in regard to water.*

*Also, there are fights over at church all the time. There is a different church that has been established, Czech Brethren. It's Protestant or Hussite. But I stayed with the old faith, Roman Catholic—where I was born, I want to stay there.*

*The money you sent converts to 720 crowns.*

*God Bless you for this. I greet hundred times Anna and Marie* [Wencel's daughters], *and their husbands. I also greet the Jikalska family, and Kacenka and Karlicek, their husbands.*

*Please write back a few lines; who is living and who has died.*

*You must forgive me that I've written this badly; I have a hard time seeing.* [Katerina's once impeccable cursive penmanship had since waned.] *Above all, my thanks to John Burich. I greet him a hundred times and send kisses.*

*I've changed my apartment; I don't live there; our landlord has died, so it's up for sale.*

*Katerina Buresova,*
*Caslav, Bohemia*

The letter revealed a few insights into evolving family dynamics.

Clearly, Katerina did not know that sisters Anna and Marie, known formally as Mary, had laid their father, Wencel, to rest one year earlier. The sisters just picked up the gift giving in their father's stead to their impoverished aunt Katerina, who was well into her eighties.

They also made no mention of their father's demise.

Also, Katerina had lost track that her niece Anna married John Burich years earlier. Had she known, she would have simply thanked her niece, who now was known as Mrs. John Burich. Even though Katerina was losing touch with current family events, she still vividly recalled all the neighbors who made their way to America.

Anna and John Burich were married in 1906. Anna's aunt Katerina, who lived in the Czech Republic and was in failing health, had lost track of family matters based on letters sent between the family members. *Author's collection.*

## The Immigrant Pledge

These letters reveal intricate insight into an immigrant family. In many ways, this situation is not much different than today's struggles. Immigrants leave troubling economic situations in search of hope and opportunity.

Those who find good fortune send money back home to support family members. In the United States, such is the case with people from Mexico and Central America. The Middle East has countless residents from the Philippines doing the same, based on this author's work travels.

While some people flee poverty, others simply run from horrible circumstances. In the 1800s, immigrants like Wencel Satorie could get land for low payments thanks to the Homestead Act signed into law by President Abraham Lincoln in 1862.

These days, entry-level jobs give immigrants a chance to work for pay far better than any option they have back home. This indeed makes America the land of opportunity and still makes the American Dream possible.

# 4

# THE STATE BANK OF WENCEL

By all accounts, Wencel Satorie wasn't a rich man when he left Bohemia and came to America in 1873. In fact, the thirty-three-year-old man was on the verge of being downright poor like many other European immigrants of that era.

Known by his Bohemian friends as Václav, the immigrant had a strong work ethic and the innate ability to pinch pennies. You might say he was a tightwad.

Wencel was industrious, yet frugal. Combined with his faith-based concern for his fellow man, this eventually allowed the first-generation American to become one of the most astute and generous businessmen in his area.

How do we know?

Wencel kept a detailed ledger written in his native Bohemian language.

## FORGED OUT WITH LITTLE TO HIS NAME

At thirty-three years of age, Wencel landed in America with his sixty-year-old mother, Mary; his thirty-one-year-old wife, Anna; and young daughters Caroline and Mary. He likely also had a few steamer trunks of clothes and family possessions.

That was it.

Heck, he was so short on cash that, on arriving in Manitowoc County, Wencel lived with his brother for four years before gathering enough money for the down payment on a forty-acre parcel of land. When Wencel finally built his house, he convinced neighbor Frank Kubale to drill well for water on the property line so both could share the expense.

Wencel's farm on the Rock was in the driest part of the township due to its shallow soils. The farm located on the rock outcropping had its own microclimate. While dry during the summer, the Niagara Escarpment's bedrock below heated the soil much earlier than the surrounding land area in the spring, allowing seeds to germinate two to three weeks before neighboring lands. That early warming of the soil allowed earlier vegetable sales. Wencel capitalized on this, as it was a very profitable venture.

But how does a man like this go from near penniless to loaning out thousands of dollars by the time of his death in 1920?

That's a darn good question. It's not like he didn't have mouths to feed.

Like many immigrants, Wencel would endure many hardships: his eldest daughter, Caroline, died at ten years old, and he would also outlive his wife by fifteen years.

However, it was Wencel's get-up-and-go that yielded him bountiful profits from his little forty-acre farm.

Like many pioneer farmers of the day, Wencel grew wheat. That was Wisconsin's leading crop before W.D. Hoard, founder of *Hoard's Dairyman* magazine, began writing about the merits of dairy farming to the immigrant masses.

Hoard was so successful in this endeavor that Wisconsin's citizens elected him the state's sixteenth governor in 1888. Years later, Wisconsin would earn the moniker "America's Dairyland," which stands to this very day.

Wencel also raised peas, oats, rye, clover and tobacco, harvested maple syrup and sold firewood from his acreage. He also built furniture and constructed all the buildings on his homestead.

Wencel recorded his finances and most important life in the *Pierce's Memorandum and Account Book*, published in 1887. His daughter Anna preserved the ledger, which gives insight to some of those crops and his ability to become one of the area's first bankers lending both money and seed to others.

As he was a private man, only Wencel's daughter Anna saw this ledger during his lifetime.

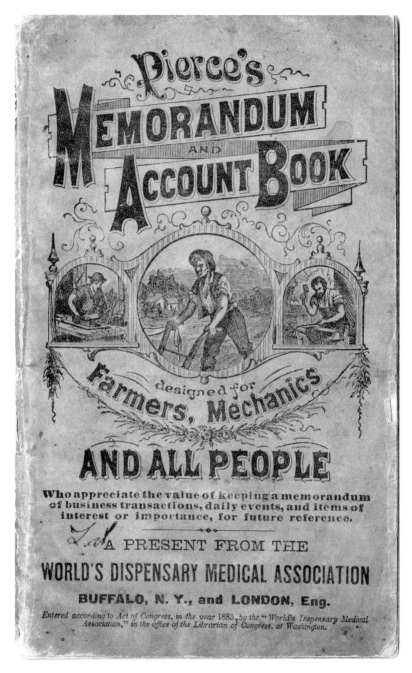

It was in this *Pierce's Memorandum and Account Book*, published in 1887, that Wencel recorded his loans. *Author's collection.*

## CROP RECORDS

"Threshed 129 bushels of grain on 19 of October [1888] and sold 8 bushels," Wencel wrote in cursive Czech in his 1887 entry in *Pierce's Memorandum and Account Book*. "On 19 of October sowed 6 bushels of rye," Wencel wrote in the European style of listing the date before the month.

That first entry clearly was the launch point for Wencel as he began tracking his business. Wencel filled that twenty-page ledger with business records until 1908.

"October 1888, I gave Tikalsky $30 dollars," entered Wencel.

"Gave to Kravic 4 bushels of peas, 12 bushels of wheat, and 12 bushels of peas. Gave him 2 maple syrups, 24 maple trees, 7 cords of wood, 1 cord of oak-pine, 2 cords of maple," wrote the then forty-eight-year-old man. Mind you, Wencel had no living sons to assist with farm work or making 10 cords of wood cut with a handsaw and hand-split with an axe. Wencel was hard at work building his business.

"On 13 of May, 1889, lent to Buresh [now spelled Burich] 6 bushels of oats and 3 bushels of wheat," wrote the farmer accountant. Wencel's daughter Anna would marry into that Burich family seventeen years later.

## THE $1,500 LOAN

"On May 29, 1889, lent the Bureshes [Buriches] $1,500 and Joe Jerabek, $16," he penned.

According to family records on the Burich side of the family, that big $1,500 loan was made to build the grandest barn in the area. That barn later housed the family's dairy herd generations later.

As America's Dairyland blossomed, many similar barns were built. These barn constructions fueled the lime kiln industry, as cement mix had yet to be perfected. Lime mortar was the bonding agent that held stone wall foundations in place for these pioneer barns.

"In 1889, I sold to Satoryova [likely his brother Tomas Satorie] 17 bushels of wheat; Kubalova [Kubale] 6 bushels wheat, and to Kranekova [likely Joseph Krause] 18 bushels of wheat.

"In 1883, on May 28, I gave to Fogeltan Tikalsky $92," he wrote in a back entry well out of order—four years before the ledger was even printed. Eventually, Wencel's only other living daughter, Mary, would marry Fogeltan's son, Joseph, ten years later on January 17, 1893.

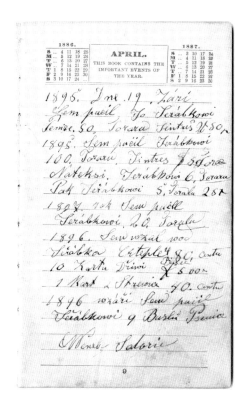

In keeping an impeccable ledger, Wencel Satorie could track his loans of money, seed, food and firewood. These entries took place in 1895. *Author's collection.*

"On 19 September, 1895, I borrowed Jerabek $50 and interest. Later that year, I borrowed to Jerabek $100 at 5 percent interest. In 1896, I lent Jerabek $20. Later in 1896, I lent another $20. Also, I lent him 9 bushels of wheat."

Based on ledger entries, Joe Jerabek, who farmed catty-corner on a forty-acre parcel diagonal from Wencel, had fallen on hard times. The Jerabek family barn burned down after Joe's son failed to properly extinguish a cigarette, according to stories passed down through the generations.

Noting the value of firewood in those days, "I got $4.80 per cord of fire wood and sold 10 cords to Jerabek."

Then, there was a dry spell in Wencel's lending to others for a span. Perhaps subpar crop yields contributed to the lower lending patterns. But there's another possibility—his wife, Anna, had fallen ill and he and his single daughter, Anna, were caring for their wife-mother and that effort was consuming much of their time.

After that eight-year lull, lending picked up once again: "On 2 February, 1903, I lent to Albert Burich, $250. On 11 September, I lent to Kubalova [Kubale] $450. 1903, on 25 of November, borrowed to Novak $100."

## TWO UNIQUE ENTRIES

Wencel also entered a bit of family history into the ledger.

"On 5 May 1905, my wife Anna died. We buried her at St. Mary's Cemetery," he wrote.

Then came a joyous day Wencel made note of in his ledger.

"On 10 June 1906, my dear daughter Anna Satori married John Burich," he wrote.

Just days prior to that union, Wencel broke with social order. On June 1906, Wencel sold his forty-acre homestead farm for one dollar to "Anna Satorie, a single lady."

There were likely a number of reasons for that transfer.

First, and foremost, Anna was very good with money. She learned financial savviness from Wencel, as he had no sons to teach. Second,

Wencel Satorie was so pleased that his daughter Anna was marrying John Burich, he had this portrait made on the same day as the couple's wedding photo. *Author's collection.*

many people still had outstanding loans with her father, and it would be Anna's job to eventually collect the money or forgive the debt. Third, she cared for her *Otec*, or "father" in the Bohemian language, for the ensuing fifteen years after her *Matka* or mother, Anna, left the earth in 1905.

It was likely a combination of all three that resulted in her Otec, Václav, breaking from centuries of culture in essentially gifting that property to Anna.

## THE FIRST WOMAN LANDOWNER

In that transaction, his hardworking and dedicated Anna became Rockland Township's first woman to own land not through the death of a husband. Anna's name would be on that property for the rest of her life, from 1906 to 1951. Although "Anna" would not be recorded in plat books, the name "Mrs. John A. Burich" appeared in every publication. She eventually willed that property to her four living daughters.

Her youngest daughter, Julia, and her husband, Elmer Pritzl, eventually bought it outright. In 2006, Anna's great-grandson proposed to his bride on that very property.

There is no doubt the well-educated Anna, both from a formal school education and from her father, brought the same methodical accounting principles to her marriage and formed a great partnership with the industrious John Burich. John vastly expanded the farmstead, and Anna kept the ledgers.

## AND WHAT OF THE STATE BANK OF WENCEL?

Reedsville eventually opened the Reedsville State Bank on October 25, 1906, with $10,000 in assets. Not one of the families who owed money to Wencel was among the shareholders—neither was Wencel, according to the book *History of Reedsville to 1976.*

Why buy stock in a bank when Wencel had his own lending business?

Plus there was the matter that banks got robbed. On October 22, 1909, the Reedsville State Bank's safe door was blown open and $6,600 was taken from its vault.

In the meantime, Wencel's loans were secure. It would be his daughter Anna's job to collect the $3,200-plus in outstanding loans recorded in that ledger.

Eventually, John and Anna Burich would open an account at the Reedsville State Bank in 1932 with a deposit of $11.75.

## LIVED TO SEE THE GOLDEN JUBILEE

According to St. Mary's Church archives, Wencel is one of four pioneers to partake in its 50th Golden Jubilee and had an audience with Green Bay's Bishop Rhode on November 11, 1915. Also there that day in the village of Reedsville were fellow pioneers Frank Hlavack, Father Vondracek and Frank Burich. While not on the official rolls of donors for the church building, Wencel, along with his daughter Anna and son-in-law John, donated red oak logs from their woods to build church pews.

So why did Wencel help others by lending?

Perhaps the worn pages in Wencel's Bohemian Bible falling open to a particular passage due to wear shed light on the matter. When translated, that passage in the Gospel of Matthew 22:37–39 reads: "Jesus said unto him,

Eventually, Wencel Satorie's farmstead fell into disrepair. Even though the farm buildings are gone, the land has been farmed by four successive generations. *Author's collection.*

thou shalt love the Lord thy God with all thy heart, and with all thy soul, and with all thy mind. This is the first and great commandment. And the second is like unto it, thou shalt love thy neighbor as thyself. On these two commandments hang all the law and the prophets."

Wencel may have ended up doing more for a "good neighbor policy" than he was rewarded with here on earth. After spending hours poring through Wencel's notes, the song "It Is Well with My Soul" began playing in my head throughout the day. And with that I believe all is well with Wencel's soul, for he helped his fellow man throughout his life in their hour of need.

The family farm and her soul were again conversing generations later.

# 5

# FIRE UP THE KILNS

Lime is one of the oldest chemicals produced by man," wrote Howard Kanetzke in the autumn 1969 issue of *Wisconsin Trails*. "Stone age men manufactured it; Egyptians plastered their pyramids with it; Aztecs and Incas raised their stone temples with it."

Lime is a principal source of calcium. The product has been so important to human civilization that most ancient languages have a word for calcium oxide.

In Latin, lime is *calx*, from which the name of the element calcium is derived. Of course, Ca now holds position 20 on the periodic table.

America's Dairyland was built on a limestone foundation, as it provided the mortar that held stone together for all the barns that dotted the rural countryside following Wisconsin governor W.D. Hoard's transformation of the Badger State from a wheat to a dairy state.

Farmers also purchased lime to whitewash barns and sheds for sanitary purposes—primarily to kill tuberculin, which causes tuberculosis, or TB. That deadly zoonotic disease could transfer from cows to humans.

One such product was Milk of Magnesia lime from the Rockwood Quarry located between Manitowoc and Two Rivers.

That same lime could also help "sweeten" land before planting and adjust the soil's pH so that perennial legume crops, such as alfalfa or clover, could survive the winter and grow multiple years. Alfalfa and clover were important forages for the state's growing dairy herds. Experiments in spreading lime on fields eventually landed the historic Hoard's Dairyman Farm in the National Register of Historic Places by the U.S. Department of the Interior.

Lime proved to be a pivotal soil amendment in helping alfalfa overwinter. W.D. Hoard conducted some of the world's very first experiments applying lime to soil to change the pH. *Hoard's Dairyman.*

Perhaps most importantly, builders purchased large quantities of Wisconsin lime to lay brick and stone walls before cement mix came upon the scene. "And when the exterior walls were completed on homes, finishing crews coated the interior walls with smooth plaster made from lime, fine sand, water, and hair," noted Kanetzke.

In other instances, lime was turned into buffing compounds for metal finishing for chrome plating, nickel and brass finishing and other uses, wrote William J. Tills in a publication called *The County Mining Industry.* Much of it was used to brighten the finish of automobile parts, toasters, irons and other household gadgets. It also was used in paper making. In addition, untreated limestone was crushed and used for building highway and railroad beds.

## Lime Kilns Sprouted Like Mushrooms

In Northeast Wisconsin, High Cliff, Greenleaf, Hayton, Grimms, Brillion, Valders, Quarry and Rockwood all had lime kilns. Wisconsin's most extensive lime operations developed near Lake Michigan, where the underlying bedrock, Niagara Dolomite, proved to be an excellent, all-purpose stone. In

USDA's 1938 aerial photography shows the extensive Grimms quarry complete with company-owned housing for employees. *USDA and the Arthur Robinson Map Library at the University of Wisconsin–Madison.*

some fields, rock ledges popped to the surface. In other places, the Niagara Dolomite lay buried under shallow layers of clay soils once found on the bottom of prehistoric lakes.

Brillion's Ormsby Lime Company opened in 1880 and exclusively manufactured quicklime. By 1885, the Ormsby Lime Company had produced 218,000 barrels of 99 percent pure quicklime, shipping over 2,000 railroad carloads from Brillion's plant that year.

The Grimms quarry, owned by the Cook and Brown Lime Company, focused on quicklime and the sale of rock for construction. The lime kilns of Grimms were such a booming business that by 1900 the little hamlet boasted 250 residents. Many of the immigrants and their adult children who worked in the lime kilns lived in onsite company housing. Viewing the first aerial photographs taken about 1938 by the United States Department of Agriculture (USDA), one can see the Grimms quarry, onsite housing and railroad activity.

Those 1938 images prove to be quite fascinating. While most Americans didn't have their eyes on the brewing war in Europe, President Roosevelt knew he needed to prepare his country.

One such project involved a 1937–41 aerial photography effort by the USDA to map fields. Certainly the project documented farm fields to implement the conservation programs passed by Congress. However, this New Deal project also assisted in training pilots to take photos during reconnaissance missions during the war.

Wisconsin's thirty-eight thousand historic images have been preserved by the Wisconsin State Cartographers Office and are stored at the Arthur H. Robinson Map Library within the Department of Geography at the University of Wisconsin–Madison.

These days, Grimms is essentially a ghost town as its sole significant employer is long gone. With the quarries shuttered, the railroad disappeared as well. That wasn't the case a century ago. In 1900, Wisconsin ranked third in the nation in lime production, as America was on its way to becoming an industrial powerhouse.

Wisconsin remained a major lime producer through the Roaring Twenties. Then construction plummeted during the Great Depression, and demand for lime dropped substantially. By 1940, scarcely 1 percent of the nation's lime came from Badger State kilns, as production moved to larger quarries in the western United States and Canada.

## FIRE! FIRE! FIRE!

Shouts rang out throughout the quarry warning everyone to take cover.

To feed the kilns with limestone, crews of workmen drilled rows of holes about five inches across vertically into the rock roughly two feet back from the cliff face. Each hole was filled with black gunpowder; when ignited, it produced enough force to open long, straight cracks in the rock. Those holes then were refilled, this time with heavy charges of dynamite. "Moments after the fuses were lit, the quarry walls echoed thundering dynamite blasts as stone pried loose came crashing to the crater floor below," wrote Kanetzke.

Grimms, a village with 250 people, sprouted when the Union Lime Company's lime kilns (later the Western Lime Company) started operating. *Photographer Ernest Francis Burchard, United States Geological Survey.*

Raw limestone needs temperatures that reach 1,800 to 2,000 degrees Fahrenheit. That was the reason the fire-driven kilns were built. During the heat treatment, carbon dioxide, vegetable matters, moisture and other impurities were driven off. If too hot, the limestone turned yellow, creating an inferior product. Wood and coal were the principal fuels in the kilns, and Wisconsin's immigrant farmers readily supplied wood.

"Our family sold firewood to the Grimms' Western Lime Company," noted Albert Burich and Wencel Satorie's granddaughter Julia. "My grandpas, Albert and Wencel, and my dad, John Burich, hauled firewood with horses and received seventy-five cents a cord."

That would be just one of our family's direct ties to the limestone industry.

# 6

# THE LIME BARON COMETH

J.W. Ormsby and O.W. Robertson of Milwaukee controlled the largest single-site lime kiln in Wisconsin's early days. That quarry, based in Grafton, Wisconsin, began operation in 1874 under the name Ormsby Lime Company, and it turned out twenty-five barrels of lime per day. That was just a dusting of the forthcoming lime production.

By 1880, that company had opened its plant just north of Spring Creek (Brillion). The lime kilns of Grimms quickly followed. Lime was in large demand, and the railroad could ship it throughout North America and beyond. With lime becoming big business, scouts were out looking to secure more limestone deposits. In 1883, lime baron O.W. Robinson traveled down a dirt road just off the Manitowoc-Menasha trail now known as U.S. Highway 10. That dirt road, less than two miles from the Milwaukee Lake Shore & Western Railroad Company's rail line (later known as the Chicago and Northwestern Railway Company) between Brillion and Reedsville, took Robinson to the immigrant home of Albert Burich, age forty-three, and his wife, Josephina, age twenty-seven.

The southwest corner of the Burich homestead had a fine limestone ledge located very close to a township roadbed. O.W. Robinson, a Milwaukee businessman, offered $300—$100 an acre—for a three-acre portion of the forty-acre homestead located on the western portion of what is known by the locals as the Rock, just west of Reedsville.

It was only sixteen years earlier that the Burich family had paid $235 for what became the forty-acre Burich family farm. With $300 for just three of the forty acres, the couple would be out of debt.

In 1883, Albert and Josephina Burich sold off a small three-acre section of the family homestead to O.W. Robinson, who planned to develop a lime quarry. *Author's collection.*

Robinson likely also knew that situation after inspecting land transfer records at the Manitowoc County Courthouse. Those records were public information. High-end prospectors such as Robinson did their homework before making any business proposal.

For Albert and Josephina, the decision to sell was made easier by the fact that Albert's father, Thomas, had died on November 25, 1882, and his mother, Mary, died two weeks later. Now Albert was solely in charge of the decision, and he would not hurt his parents' feelings by selling a small portion of the family homestead. The money would be a blessing; the couple had five young children.

On April 23, 1883, O.W. Robinson purchased the property with one condition stated on the deed: "Be it understood that first parties have the first right to purchase premises if offered for sale." That first party noted on the abstract of title was Albert Burich and his direct descendants.

Just twelve years after its purchase, the property was transferred to the Hayton Lime Works. By 1890, it had been sold to the Ormsby Lime Company. By 1902, it had been sold to the Union Lime Company. And in

1921, it was sold to the Western Lime and Cement Company. With that sale, the Brillion and Grimms quarries were owned by the same company. As O.W. Robinson held a share in each of these companies, that sale kept the deed restriction in place with the Burich family.

## Was It Good Lime?

"My dad, Louis Pritzl Sr., said, 'the lime company in Brillion was wondering whether the lime on the Rock was any good,'" recalled Elmer Pritzl, who would enter the family tree after marrying Albert's granddaughter Julia.

"In those days, they didn't have cement. It wasn't available yet. They used lime mortar to hold brick and stone together," said Elmer. Since the couple had taken over the farm, they were among the direct descendants referred to in the abstract of title. They also were the fourth generation to run the family farm.

"My dad, Louis, said the Brillion-based lime quarry sent out four men, two teams of horses and two wagons," continued Elmer, whose father was a local mason and knew a great deal about mortaring stone and brick. "The lime company's men set dynamite to get some rock loose. They loaded it and hauled it to Brillion with the four horses. All agreed it was good stone after running it through the kiln.

"But a few years later along came cement, and the lime kiln days would come to an end," continued Elmer. If the Brillion and Grimms quarries ever ran out of rock, O.W. Robinson would have started the new quarry in rural Reedsville. For that to happen, his company and its agents would have to convince the area's farming families to sell more land. Those pioneers included the Becker, Burich, Haelfrisch, Krueger, Kubale, Rusch, Satorie and Schmidt families, who all owned land on the Rock and its limestone-fortified land mass.

## Rockland Had Its Own Quarry

In addition to the Robinson claim, Rockland Township had a small quarry on the southeast section of the Rock. That quarry was situated between the Haelfrisch and Krueger family homesteads.

"The Town of Rockland eventually owned that quarry for a number of decades," said Tim Thor, owner of Hilltop Trucking and Excavating. "Back in the day, Alfred Schroeder and his wife, Nadia, born a Kinast, owned Schroeder Excavating. Alfred hauled crushed gravel from that quarry for Rockland Township roads and other local townships," explained Thor, who now owns the property site.

"In the 1940s, as oral history has it, the town installed a steam engine on that site," he added. "The steam engine ran a winch that pulled trolley cars…like ones you would see on a train tracks for a western mine. Once at the top of the quarry, that same steam engine would crush the limestone," said Thor.

This was the same crushing process that took place in many lime quarries with kilns. After the rock was blasted from the lime walls by dynamite, it was placed into a crusher. There, pieces from a few inches to two to three feet in diameter were cracked open like eggshells and pounded into one-, two- and three-inch rock pieces resembling gravel. A five-ton steam-driven jaw did all the work.

Once prepared, that limestone became the base for the town's roads.

"That continued throughout the 1940s and 1950s," said Thor.

After that, the quarry was converted into the township's dump. Years later, the Wisconsin Department of Natural Resources (DNR) shut down the dump and asked that the township clean up the site, as its rock base could allow contaminants to flow into the groundwater.

Knowing the Rockland Township had no use for the quarry, Thor asked town leaders if he could purchase the site. Permission was granted if Thor cleaned up the quarry to the satisfaction of DNR officials. Thor completed the cleanup and purchased the site. The property now stores busted concrete and stone with the long-term goal of crushing it once again for a second useful life.

## Back in Burich Hands

Even though Wisconsin's booming lime kiln era had long come to a close by the end of World War II, businessmen hung on to land claims hoping for limestone's return to its once profitable past.

By 1965, the writing was on the wall and the Western Lime and Cement Company was looking to divest some of its assets. An executive had his eyes

Rosalie and Randy Geiger stand near the limestone ledge purchased by O.W. Robinson in 1883. In 1965, Rosalie's parents, Elmer and Julia (Burich) Pritzl, reacquired the land from the Western Lime and Cement Company. *Author's collection.*

on the three-acre parcel on the company's unopened Reedsville quarry site. That executive wanted to build a home there, as those limestone outcroppings would create a perfect setting. However, one item on the deed had to be resolved: "Be it understood that first parties have the first right to purchase premises if offered for sale."

The Western Lime and Cement Company was legally bound to find out if Albert and Josephina Burich had any heirs. It didn't take long to learn that Albert had a granddaughter, Julia, still milking cows in the same barn that Albert had milked in nearly eighty years earlier.

"The Western Lime and Cement Company wanted $600 for the three acres...after owning it for eighty-two years," recalled Julia during a 2006 interview. "We agreed to buy back the three acres over the phone to fully restore the family homestead," she said. "My grandpa Albert Burich would have been pleased to get the land back."

That land sale back to the family of the original owners ended the prospect of a Reedsville limestone quarry.

Wisconsin's lime business had gone full circle—from boom to bust.

# 7

# THE CHEESEHEADS ARE BORN

As lime kilns were booming, so, too, was cheese. However, unlike the lime business, cheese never went bust; it just boomed louder and louder, growing right along with Wisconsin's dairy herds' skyrocketing milk production.

"I want to present you with Cheesehead awards," declared "Cheddar McFarley," mayor of the fictitious town "Cheeseopolis."

"Edgar 'Cheddarhead' Bennett I declare you Cheesehead Honorary."

"Andre 'The Brie' Rison," continued Mayor Cheddar McFarley, known to most people as the world-renowned comedian Chris Farley, "you were great."

"Sean 'The String Cheese' Jones" said Farley, "thank you for returning the title to America's Dairyland." And with that, Farley placed the final foam Cheesehead on the three Green Bay Packers players who appeared on *The Tonight Show with Jay Leno* just one day after defeating the New England Patriots to win Super Bowl XXXI one day earlier on January 28, 1996.

At this point, Leno was laughing so hard he was crying.

Cheeseheads.

That term, more than any other, instantly signals that the person is either from Wisconsin or that they follow the Green Bay Packers.

Wisconsin wasn't always the land of cheese. But, once the Badger State earned the title, it never looked back. Today, Wisconsin produces nearly 30 percent of the nation's cheese. More importantly, its 130-plus cheese plants and their 1,200-plus licensed cheesemakers produce over 600 varieties of specialty cheese—that's more varieties than all of Europe.

Wisconsin's cheesemaking prowess is like wine to France or beer to Belgium.

The "Seven Wise Men" gave rise to Wisconsin's dairy industry. Hoard led the charge, and Hazen pursued the then outlandish idea of building a cheese factory. *Hoard's Dairyman.*

## DAIRY'S EPICENTER

In 1871, a quiet, but steady drumbeat started reverberating from southern Wisconsin. That's when William Dempster Hoard founded the first county-based dairymen's association nestled midway between Madison and Milwaukee in Jefferson County. By the very next year, the beat had become a steady thump as W.D. Hoard went on to lead a group known as the "seven

Farmers from around the world quickly embraced Dr. Stephen Babcock's test to measure butterfat and more precisely price milk. Babcock is shown far right. *Hoard's Dairyman.*

wise men" who founded the Wisconsin Dairyman's Association. In addition to Hoard were Chester Hazen, Stephen and A.D. Favill, H.C. Drake, Walter Greene and H.F. Dousman.

Chester Hazen built Wisconsin's first cheese plant in 1864. It was initially known as "Hazen's Folly." But no one was laughing a few years later as fifty more plants popped up by the close of that decade.

As he was the leader of the group, Hoard's mission was simple—transform the Badger State from a one-crop wheat system that had been eroding its fragile glacial soils into a dairy empire. As dairy cow numbers climbed rapidly, the New York native knew full well that his adopted Badger State would need to export its number one agricultural product—cheese—to the nation's major population centers.

So, in 1873, Hoard secured the first refrigerator train car to ship Wisconsin cheese east. From that point, Wisconsin pioneers built more cheese factories and its reputation for cheese grew.

However, Hoard was just getting started. Over the next fifteen years, the father of Wisconsin's dairy industry started:

- an international dairy publication reaching readers in over one hundred countries
- the University of Wisconsin–Madison's College of Agriculture
- North America's first dairy science program for milk production
- North America's first dairy products and food science program
- North America's first genetics program

Hoard became Wisconsin's sixteenth governor, but his biggest achievement just may have been recruiting Stephen Babcock from the nation's leading dairy state of the day—New York. Once in Wisconsin, the former Cornell University scientist developed a test to measure butterfat just as Hoard would end his term as governor in 1890.

The famed Babcock test became the gold standard to measure butterfat. Almost overnight, the Babcock test standardized milk pricing throughout Wisconsin and eventually the world.

By the turn of the century, Wisconsin had 1,500 cheese factories located at major rural crossroads. By 1922, that number swelled to over 2,800 cheese factories.

In just four decades, Wisconsin overtook New York to become the nation's leading dairy state for both milk and cheese production. Lawmakers were so proud of the burgeoning dairy economy the state legislature affixed the phrase "America's Dairyland" to the state's license plates in 1939.

## THE CORNER CHEESE FACTORY

John and Anna Burich shipped their milk to the Round Lake Dairy owned by A.B. Neumann. Milk was taken in cans to the factory located at the intersection of modern-day Manitowoc and Long Lake Roads.

By the time of her husband's passing in 1939, finances were constantly on Anna Burich's mind; she saved every bi-monthly pay stub that year. This detailed collection of twenty-four milk check statements provides an incredible snapshot into dairy markets of the day.

PEAK MILK. The May 16 to June 1 handwritten ledger indicates the Burich farm shipped 7,217 pounds of milk. That was about 20 pounds per cow for the 23 hand-milked cows. During that same window, the Round Lake Dairy took in 150,875 pounds of milk. That meant Anna Burich accounted for about 5 percent of the cheese factory's intake. The butterfat was 3.2 percent for the Burich milk, while the entire plant was 3.5.

—FOR YOUR HEALTH—
EAT MORE WISCONSIN CHEESE

Statement of
**ROUND LAKE DAIRY**
A. B. NEUMANN, Prop.

From *May 16* to *June* 19*39*
Total Milk *150,875*
Average Test *3.5*
Total Fat *5298.113*
Price of Fat per lb. *.315*
Ave. Price per cwt. of Milk *1.10*
Price per cwt. of 4% Milk *1.26*
Amt. of Milk brought by you *7217*
Your Test *3.2*
Price per cwt. of your Whey and Milk *1.008*
Amount due you *72.74*
Price of Cheese *13/2 + 13*
Trucking Charge *3.61*
Amount of Cheese sold to you *C.C. = .10*

Amount of Butter sold to you *2 = .50*
Gas
Oil

Your Debit *4.21*
Cash enclosed to you *34.27 + 34.26*
Name of Patron *Mrs. J. a. Burrich*
*George Rubsch*

—FOR YOUR HEALTH—
EAT MORE WISCONSIN CHEESE

Statement of
**ROUND LAKE DAIRY**
A. B. NEUMANN, Prop.

From *Dec. 1* to *16* 19*39*
Total Milk *37,318*
Average Test *3.89*
Total Fat *1446.914*
Price of Fat per lb. *.385*
Ave. Price per cwt. of Milk *1.489*
Price per cwt. of 4% Milk *1.54*
Amt. of Milk brought by you *1393*
Your Test *4.2*
Price per cwt. of your Whey and Milk *1.617*
Amount due you *22.52*
Price of Cheese *15/2*
Trucking Charge *.70*
Amount of Cheese sold to you *.12*

Amount of Butter sold to you *1 = .31*
Gas
Oil

Your Debit *1.13*
Cash enclosed to you *21.63 =*
Name of Patron *Mrs. J. a. Burrich*

*Left*: The May 16 to June 1, 1939 handwritten pay envelope from Round Lake Dairy, A.B. Neumann, proprietor. Mrs. John Burich received $72.74 for 7,217 pounds of milk. *Author's collection.*

*Right*: Late winter months represented the low tide in milk production. The Burich herd produced only 1,393 pounds of milk in the final two weeks of the year. *Author's collection.*

The pay stubs indicated that A.B. Neumann procured 153,424 pounds of milk the next two weeks of 1939 from June 1 to June 16, while Anna shipped 6,565 pounds of that total. Again, the Burich farm's butterfat was a bit lower than the plant total at 3.3 versus 3.5 percent. She earned one dollar for every 100 pounds of milk.

JUNE DAIRY MONTH. Cheese plants swelled with milk in June as cows grazed rich pastures. Every farm was fenced from property line to property line.

In order to stabilize dairy demand during peak production periods, the National Dairy Council supported National Milk Month from June 10 to July 10.

The National Dairy Council officially changed the name of its marketing effort to June Dairy Month in 1939. The very next year, Wisconsin governor

Julius Heil proclaimed the state's first June Dairy Month. We've been celebrating June Dairy Month ever since.

Low MILK TIDE. With declining daylight and the only feed stored grains and forages, milk production slid as the year went along. Milk flow hit its low water mark from December 1 to December 16, when the Round Lake Dairy took in only 37,318 pounds of milk. That was 24 percent of June's peak milk flow.

To encourage shipments, pay prices were higher in the winter months. For her 1,393 pounds of milk, Anna earned $1.62 for every 100 pounds that December. With stored feedstuffs as the main ration source, butterfat climbed to 4.2 percent. Higher butterfat milk yielded more butter and cheese.

EXTRA CHARGES. At one time, farmers hauled their own milk. Eventually, milk routes took root and truckers transported several farmers' milk cans to the cheese factory.

From June 1 to June 16, Anna paid $3.28 to the trucker. That was deducted from her milk check. She also purchased $0.35 worth of cheese, $0.10 of cottage cheese and $0.51 worth of butter—25.5 cents per pound. In those days, it was regular practice for the cheese plant to sell dairy products to its patrons.

Once the deductions were determined by A.B. Neumann, an envelope held a cash settlement for the patron's milk. Yes, cash was the payment, as no one trusted banks due to the market crash earlier that decade. It's these envelopes that served as a foundation for this story.

## A DAIRY RENAISSANCE

The word *renaissance* means "rebirth" or "revival." Wisconsin is now experiencing a renaissance where dairy producers and processors alike are reinvesting in America's Dairyland—even through these troubling economic times for dairy farmers.

While the number of cheese factories had declined dramatically, there has been a rebirth. Wisconsin has realized that value added cheese sales brings opportunity.

Today the state produces over six hundred types of cheese, with more on the way. This revolution that gave rise to America's Dairyland and this newfound renaissance does indeed make us the land of Cheeseheads. The Burich family and its dairy herd helped contribute to the land of cheese.

# 8

# LET'S MOVE THE HOMESTEAD HOUSE

Travel is plush these days. While it's true there might be delays due to construction or weather, for the most part, we travel in style.

That wasn't the case when people emigrated from Europe in the 1800s. After crossing the Atlantic Ocean, which was a choppy and somewhat dangerous trek, immigrants still had to journey across the United States to arrive to their destination.

Then consider after that ocean voyage you still did not have a place to call home.

Once settlers arrived and found a plot of land, all immediate attention focused on quickly providing your family with two of life's three major necessities—food and shelter. Clothes, the third necessity, could wait a bit because immigrants at least arrived with the clothes on their backs along with a few items held in steamer trunks.

Food took top priority in spring. After getting seeds in the soil, building a log cabin was the next priority because the cold Wisconsin winter soon would be bearing down on the immigrants.

That being the case, hasty decisions were sometimes made on site selection. Such was the case with the Burich family who homesteaded in the Rockland Township, just west of Reedsville, in 1867.

# THE FIRST FLAT SITE

Prior to homesteading, loggers often stripped the land of its trees in a process known as clear-cut logging. That took place on our family homestead as sawmills sprouted up throughout the area like dandelions on a spring lawn.

Settlers then cleared the aftermath—stumps—from the land, starting with the best soil. In the case of the Burich family, that just so happened to be in a location far from any road. That didn't matter though because early residents often rode horses or drove horse teams through neighbors' fields en route to town, especially in winter when pulling sleighs.

However, as Wisconsin transitioned to America's Dairyland, up went barbed-wire fences that sectioned off much of the land to keep in cattle. Early pioneers could no longer cut across neighboring property.

At some point after his parents passed in the fall of 1882, Albert Burich determined that keeping his log cabin on the best soil limited his ability to grow wheat and clover. Also, the homestead was nearly a quarter mile from the nearest road; the roads had been gradually improved with gravel firming up the base to transport crops to the nearby Reedsville railroad depot.

That's when Albert came up with the plan to move his home.

# WHY NOT BUILD NEW?

Labor was cheap and building materials were expensive. If there was a fire, people would scrape through the ruins to salvage the nails. Plus, time was precious as one toiled to scratch out a living from the land, cut wood for winter heat and grow crops to feed cattle and put food on the table.

Those were the prevailing economic conditions of the day.

Moving a log cabin across half of a forty-acre parcel, a distance of one-eighth of a mile, would be painstakingly slow. And think back to the available resources in the late 1800s. Manpower, horsepower and some hand tools were the available options.

The process began by jacking up the house from its foundation. Screw jacks, as opposed to modern-day hydraulic jacks, were really the only option to lift the log cabin off its foundation. Multiple screw jacks would be set under the house's foundation. Timbers would be set in place vertically, and the screw jacks would be turned by hand in order to lift the house. Each jack had perpendicular holes for pipes to be installed—the heavier the object, the longer the pipe that was needed to turn the jack in order to get more leverage.

We still have those screw jacks on my parents' farm. These days those jacks seldom see use because it took time to turn them; modern-day hydraulic jacks get the job done much quicker.

Once the house was raised off its foundation, heavy wooden beams twelve inches by twelve inches in diameter and longer than the building's width were slid underneath. Next, the screw jacks were lowered until the house rested on the beams. Once firmly in position, the house was secured for transport.

After the house was in place, a temporary wooden track was laid on the ground, and the beams under the log cabin slid along greased runners. In other instances, round log rollers could be placed under the wooden beams, according to a history of Shiawassee County, Michigan, that details similar moves.

As the house slid along, the planks or rollers were removed from the rear of the house and carried to the front of the house. This process continued until the log cabin was at its new location. This could take days.


## Horse and Ox Power

Farm animals provided the power. However, it would have taken a tremendous team of animals to move the house on a straight-out pull. A capstan would have helped move the Buriches' log cabin. The capstan, which worked like a winch, was anchored to a heavy object well ahead of the house.

To paint a visual image, these were the key items:

1. A pulley was attached to the house.
2. A capstan (a revolving cylinder with a vertical axis used for winding a rope or cable) was in the middle. In other instances, an elaborate rope-and-pulley system could be deployed in lieu of a capstan.
3. A dead man anchor, typically a tree, would serve as an anchor point well in front of the house and the capstan. Heavy chain secured the capstan or a rope-and-pulley system to the tree. Referred to in the pioneer days as "burying a dead man," an object buried perpendicular to the house, such as a log, could

have served as the dead man if no tree or large rock was available for the anchor point.

4. A cable, chain or rope connected the pulley/house to the capstan. The capstan was then turned by horses or an ox team that walked in a circle and tugged on a pole or "sweep" connected to the capstan. As those animals walked repetitively in a circle, the cable would slowly wind up on the capstan and pull the house forward, inches at a time.

"It was quite a project to move a house in those days," said Albert's granddaughter Julia Burich Pritzl, as the family passed down the feat through the generations. "Pa's uncle Louis Turensky helped move it. He moved houses, barns and everything like that for people. He was quite a guy."

Louis Turensky was a familiar figure in Rockland Township and held public office for many years. Louis often helped out the Burich family, as his sister Josephina was married to Albert Burich.

In true pioneer spirit, if Louis thought it could be done, he would give it a try. "He even had a threshing machine and a sawmill," said Julia. "He sawed nearly all the lumber for buildings on the farm."

In modern times, few houses are moved. It's often easier, and far less expensive, to raze an old building and construct a new one in its place rather than to move and rehabilitate the old one.

## Set on a New Foundation

As for the Burich homestead, once it was on its new foundation, screw jacks lifted it off the beam runners and slowly lowered the log cabin into place. Given that Albert and Josephina had a growing family, an addition with pine clapboard siding was added to the front of the log cabin to give it more space and a more modern look. That home stood in its new place for the ensuing decades. By 1916, a new faced-cement block home was constructed behind the family homestead.

Even though it no longer served as the family home, that log cabin and pine-sided pioneer home stood another nine years until its lumber and timbers were stripped for a new cattle barn built. The 1860s hand-hewn logs went into the barn's main floor to support the second-story mow floor. Its boards live on as a roof for the barn.

The Burich family pioneer homestead, with its pine-sided front and log cabin rear, is shown in this early 1900s photo at the wedding of Miss Elizabeth Burich and Mr. Frank Kirch (*center*), with John Burich shown feeding the chickens. *Author's collection.*

With that deconstruction, the original homestead was no more.

As for its basement, during extremely dry summers, one can see the skeleton of the log cabin's foundation. Only a thin layer of topsoil covers the square, hollowed-out profile of its former basement. It's on that basement skeleton that grass dries up and goes dormant before the surrounding lawn.

One other remnant is the hand pump well that once sat on the southwest corner of the front porch. To this day, you can still pump it for a glass of cold water.

# 9

# THIS PRIEST WAS LIKE LOMBARDI

Think of only three things: your God, your family and the Green Bay Packers—in that order," quipped Vince Lombardi, the famed coach of the Green Bay Packers.

After unearthing some photos and newspaper clippings in the Burich and Satorie family archives, Lombardi's quote is the first thing that came to my mind when reading about a man named Frank Kolar.

So what does Kolar have in common with Lombardi?

In the often-recited quote, Lombardi was instilling priorities for life: God (faith), family, the Green Bay Packers (community)—into the men on his young football team. Despite hitting rock bottom—winning only one game in 1958—Lombardi took the helm in 1959 and convinced the group of men that they had greatness deep within. Lombardi carried out such a masterful job that Green Bay shocked the football world by winning the National Football League (NFL) title in 1961. Four more titles would follow.

Let's take a journey that has strong parallels between the NFL's most famous coach and a man known to immigrant Reedsville as Reverend Francis "Frank" Kolar.

Like Lombardi, Kolar was all about faith, family and community.

Those same life principles aligned closely with the residents of the little farming community where faith, family and the farm guided each day in the rural countryside. And make no mistake, those words and values stood in that order of importance—faith, family and farm. Faith trumped family, and family stood more important than farm. However, those three standards were bonded together as if links in the strongest of log chains.

Vince Lombardi's journey through life was very much the same as those first-generation immigrants.

Lombardi was born to Enrico "Harry" Lombardi and Matilda "Mattie" Izzo in 1913. Both Harry and Mattie's parents emigrated from Italy. Harry was one of three siblings, and Matilda came from a family of twelve. Church attendance for Vince Lombardi and his four siblings was mandatory. Subject to a great of deal ethnic discrimination as an Italian living in Brooklyn, Lombardi clung to his tightknit neighborhood connections and to his Catholic faith.

Lombardi carried those bonds with him throughout his entire life. He avidly supported holding training camps at St. Norbert's, a Catholic college in DePere. He also attended mass nearly every day of his life—even during football season on Sunday morning.

"Think of only three things: your God, your family, and the Green Bay Packers—in that order."

## REEDSVILLE FLOUNDERED

In 1896, Adalbert Cipin had a full plate upon arriving in Reedsville. Not only was St. Mary's his lead parish, but he also attended to the smaller Catholic congregations of nearby Kasson and Brillion that were mission churches of Reedsville.

With Brillion growing, Cipin went to work constructing a new church to hold the congregation. By November 30, 1899, the first church service had been held in Brillion, and Father Cipin and the Brillion congregation assumed the mission church in Kasson as the German-speaking faithful there were more closely aligned by language.

The Bohemian parish of Reedsville was entirely on its own.

It floundered.

St. Mary's of Reedsville had to support a pastor and the sisters who taught at its school all on its own. Another pastor followed Cipin, and he requested a transfer after two short years. Reedsville then went without a priest for the next eight months. Finances worsened.

What would become of the Reedsville faithful?

## THEY SENT A BOHEMIAN

The bishop handpicked Reverend Francis "Frank" Kolar. While the obstacles before him seemed insurmountable, Father Kolar approached his daunting task energetically, fearlessly and faithfully, wrote Raymond Selner in his book *The Czech Catholic Parishes in Northeast Wisconsin.*

What resources were available to Father Kolar?

There were fifty-three Bohemian families, two Irish and one German household. The congregation was nearly all from the Czech region of Europe.

That was fine for Kolar, who was born in Chrudim, Bohemia, and immigrated to America in 1887. Kolar completed his theology at St. Francis Seminary in Milwaukee, Wisconsin, after starting studies at the Catholic university in Prague prior to his arrival in America.

Like Lombardi, Kolar would not tolerate self-loathing.

"Potřebujeme nový Kostel!" said the fearless leader in Bohemian from the pulpit during a church service in the late fall of 1905. If one had been sitting in church that Sunday morning, surely those sitting in the church pews would have been in shock or disbelief because Father Kolar had just said, "We need a new church!"

Kolar created a game plan and would not take no for an answer.

On June 19, 1906, just nine months after his arrival, Father Kolar said his last mass at old St. Mary's with eighteen children receiving their First

Knights of St. George were assembled in 1905 under Father Frank Kolar. It was the Knights of St. George that dutifully helped with the demolition of the old church. *Author's collection.*

Communion on that final day. The following Monday morning, the church was emptied, and on Tuesday, Reedsville's parish families came with sledgehammers and pickaxes to raze the church.

The Buriches and Satories were among those to arrive at the demolition.

Kolar had ambition. He spread it like the apostles going forth from Jerusalem after receiving the Holy Spirit at Pentecost. Kolar made believers where, just a few years earlier, people were wallowing in self-doubt.

By June 2, 1907, the new cornerstone had been laid.

## America's First

Like Lombardi, Kolar delivered the most improbable turnaround in Reedsville.

On June 25, 1908, Bishop Fox and Bishop Koudelka led a consecration ceremony with twenty-eight additional priests serving attendees. Then Bishop Koudelka, Bishop Fox and Father Kraemer all gave sermons.

Father Kolar didn't say a word during the formal festivities that day—he didn't have to—he just completed what was improbable with the help of God and his faithful parishioners.

In America in 1909, there were 145 Czech churches, according to an article in the *Katolik Magazine*, translated by Raymond Selner. None of those Czech Catholic churches was consecrated. To be consecrated, the church had to be constructed of brick or stone, all related property had to be debt-free within a year of construction and the congregation had to be extremely devout in worship of Christ.

Kolar not only built the church but also convinced parishioners to donate $21,000 in just two years. A century later, that would be nearly $600,000. The Reedsville church had no mortgage when its neighbor Brillion still had $7,000 of debt on its new church.

In addition to cash, there was donated gravel and lumber for the new church along with the necessary labor to deconstruct the old church. As a result of Kolar's zeal, the parish added thirteen more families from 1905 to 1908 to bring the total to sixty-nine.

## Kolar Had a Track Record

Before arriving in Reedsville in 1905, Kolar had already accumulated an impressive résumé. During his rectorship at St. John's Parish, Milwaukee, from 1889 to 1891, he built a parochial school and a sisters' house known to Catholics as a convent. He built the new church at St. Mary's in Antigo during a stint from 1900 to 1902. He also served parishes in St. Paul, Minnesota; Slovan in Wisconsin's Kewaunee County; Tisch Mills and Kellnersville, both in Manitowoc County.

With all that success, where would Kolar celebrate his fiftieth year as a priest?

On April 23, 1939, Father Kolar chose Reedsville for the site of his Golden Jubilee. That day also happened to be his seventy-fourth birthday.

Co-celebrating with him that day were five former altar boys who were inspired by Kolar to become Catholic priests (locations listed as of 1939): the Reverend Dr. Charles Koudelka of Milwaukee, Wisconsin; Reverend Joseph Hlavacheck, Detroit, Michigan; Reverend Joseph Vondrachek, Stangelville, Wisconsin; Frank Svatek, Carlton, Wisconsin; and Hubert Kleiber, Brillion, Wisconsin. Sermons were delivered by Bishop Paul Rhode of Green Bay, the Reverend John Gehl of nearby Denmark and Dr. Koudelka.

## A State Chaplain

Kolar freely gave of his time, talents and treasures to his greater community. The Reverend Kolar was state chaplain of the Bohemian Catholic Central Union of Wisconsin for fifteen years, a member of the Bohemian National Council of the United States and a correspondent for the Bohemian weekly newspapers based in Chicago and St. Louis since 1887.

Following what became known as World War I, Father Kolar was a special representative on religious and political affairs to Czecho-Slovakia in 1920 and was selected by the U.S. government and the Catholic Welfare Council.

Of course, the newly created country of Czecho-Slovakia included the former Bohemia.

"The National Catholic War Council has added another important branch to its overseas reconstruction activities by it works in Czechoslovakia, a newly formed and independent republic in the heart of Europe, composed of Czechs (Bohemians), Moravians, and Silesians of the former Kingdom of Bohemia, and the Slovaks, former subjects of Hungry," wrote the editors of the National Catholic War Council in its November 1919 bulletin. "The Czechs and the Slovaks were very keen for self-government and stood solidly arrayed against the tyrannical yoke of Austria-Hungry. The World War offered the opportunity and the Czechoslovaks grasped it and are today a free nation. However, the sudden transition from one form of government to another has its natural drawbacks and difficulties."

Hence the special envoy from the National Alliance of Bohemian Catholics.

Not only was Father Frank Kolar a Roman Catholic priest, he also served his adopted America in a special envoy to war-torn Czecho-Slovakia following World War I. *Author's collection.*

At first, three representatives were sent. After several months of work, more talent was needed to help the young nation and its citizens.

The next mission included seven men from Chicago, Illinois; St. Louis, Missouri; Omaha, Nebraska; and other large urban centers. However, the group's leader hailed from the little village of Reedsville, Wisconsin, and its population of six hundred souls. Indeed, Reverend Francis "Frank" Kolar led the team that helped build a new government.

In performing this civic duty, Kolar had come full circle. He returned to his birthplace in Czechoslovakia where his father had been an Austrian army officer who was wounded years earlier at Sadova during the war between Prussia and Austria in 1866. When Kolar returned to his war-torn homeland, only three of his twelve siblings were still living: Rudolph, Eman and Catherine.

# Knights of St. George

As a young schoolboy attending weekly mass, I learned that stained-glass windows tell stories. In immigrant America, those windows helped convey Christian stories to those churchgoers who were unable to read.

One of those parish illiterates would have been John Burich, who never returned to school after the second grade. The visuals of those windows must have spoken to John, as he hung portraits of his favorite saints along with close family members throughout his new home a decade later.

There is one unique window at St. Mary's depicting St. George. St. George died in AD 303 after refusing to renounce God. George had been a member of Diocletian's army and the imperial guard for Roman emperor Nicomedia. General Diocletian hated Christians.

When Diocletian ordered George's execution, George gave his money to the poor. On April 23, 303, George was decapitated before Nicomedia's outer wall. His body was sent to Lydda for burial, and Christians honored George as a martyr. He later became a saint and role model to many throughout Europe.

A Catholic fraternal society named the Knights of St. George organized in Pittsburgh, Pennsylvania, in 1880 with the approval of Bishop John Tuigg. The purpose was to support the many German immigrant families settling in the Pittsburgh area.

The movement eventually made its way to Reedsville. It was these Knights who ushered the new church forward; John Burich proudly wore his Knights of St. George ribbon and medal on his wedding day in June 1906. As a Knight of St. George, John Burich dutifully helped with the old church's demolition and dug gravel from his quarry for its new foundation. John, his father, Albert, and his father-in-law also donated red oak logs for the church pews.

Reedsville eventually converted its Knights of St. George to the better-known Knights of Columbus; the organization serves the local parish to this day.

# Father Kolar's Team

Like every great coach, your legacy is what you leave for the next generation. By that measure, Father Kolar was a hall of famer. The following men all attended St. Mary's School of Reedsville during Father Kolar's pastorate and went on to become priests:

Monsignor Hubert Kleiber
Father Charles Koudelka
Father Joseph Vondrachek
Father Lawrence (John) Vesely
Father Francis Svatek
Father Joseph Hlavacheck
Monsignor Hubert Kleiber
Father Isadore Gosz

Of those who went on to serve God's people from the collective Brillion, Kasson, Maple Grove and Reedsville parishes that now form Holy Family Parish, eight of the nineteen priests chose their vocation under Father Kolar's tutelage. Now that's a team that Lombardi would have been proud to have coached.

# 10

# BLACK JOHN OR RED JOHN?

*John J. Burich*
*Rural Route 2*
*Reedsville, Wis.*
*Simple enough.*

That postal address should have been all it took to get a letter or, more importantly, a bill delivered to John J. Burich after the U.S. Postal Service launched its Rural Free Delivery service from the Reedsville Post Office on September 1, 1904.

But it was not that easy—there were two men named John J. Burich. Not only did both live in rural Reedsville, but they also lived on its Rural Route 2 delivery zone.

## WHY TWO JOHN J. BURICHES?

These days, most families with the same last family name would try to avoid this confusion by keeping in touch with one another when choosing names for children at birth. However, that courtesy did not happen for these distant cousins.

In the late 1800s, news traveled slowly. In all likelihood, a pioneer farm family would travel to town twice each week—on Sunday for church and perhaps one other day to conduct business. Then there was the matter that English, Bohemian, German and Irish languages were all being spoken on the streets of Reedsville. Given these communication challenges of the day, only close kinfolks or clergy knew a preschooler's name.

The first John J. Burich was born on May 13, 1877, to John and Barbara (Vesely) Burich in the family's farmstead home in the town of Rockland. As an adult, this John would marry Louise Novak in 1920.

The second John J. Burich, known to many locals as Red John, was born on April 20, 1878, to Albert and Josephina (Turensky) Burich. He is my great-grandfather and eventually married Anna Satorie in 1906.

The two Burich boys were sent to the nearby St. Mary's grade school. It's there that the two boys bearing the same name interacted on a daily basis—although the two would have been in different grades separated by eleven months of age.

The fact that there were two young boys named John J. Burich probably did not affect Catholic nuns who taught at St. Mary's all that much. That's because Albert and Josephina Burich pulled their John J. Burich out of school after the second grade; the family needed more hands to help on their family's 160-plus acre farm.

And so the problem went away until 1905.

## A Delivery Nightmare

Reedville's local business owners had long resolved the issue of addressing Reedsville's two men named John Joseph Burich. As children, the slightly older John J. had jet-black hair, while the other John had wavy auburn-red hair. These attributes carried into adulthood.

When mailing bills for services rendered, local proprietors would simply write: Black John Burich or Red John Burich. With that name written on the outside of the envelope, the letter writers would continue with Rural Route 2—or RR2 for short—and finish with Reedsville, Wisconsin. That led to an easy solution for Reedsville's postmaster.

With the right John Burich—Black or Red—identified, the postmaster could deliver the letter. Historic handwritten letters addressed to Red John Burich document this regular occurrence.

However, no government agency would use the Black John or Red John vernacular on an official document. A legal name was required, and this holds true to this very day in land transfer or declarations for public office.

Born just eleven months apart, Reedsville's two John J. Buriches caused great confusion for the postmaster and letter writers alike. "Red" John Burich (*seated*) legally changed his name to John A. Burich. *Author's collection.*

When Red John J. Burich wanted to buy his father Albert's farm, Black John Burich also became a full-time farmer about the same time on a nearby family homestead. Then tax bills started getting issued to John J. Burich. This legal document, along with other government records, caused Reedsville's postmaster's angst.

The two men in their late twenties had grown tired of the competing names matter, too. Each had to routinely exchange incorrectly delivered mail. They had to do so by horse, making the endeavor a real chore.

Hence the meeting with Louis Busse the postmaster and the resulting rather pointed question, "Would one of you just change your name?"

Louis Busse was bold enough to ask the question. After all, he was one of the village's most prominent—and for that matter, the most public-spirited—citizens of his locality, wrote the authors of *History of Manitowoc County* in 1911 and 1912 of Busse's persona.

During the meeting, Red John decided to legally change his name at the Manitowoc County Courthouse, selecting the name John Albert Burich. Everyone could quickly ascertain that John A. Burich was the son of Albert Burich while John Joseph Burich was the son of John Burich.

Reedsville's postmaster was pleased. He, his clerks and mail carriers could now do their jobs.

While some reading this story may think it is a tall tale, careful review of Mrs. John A. Burich's (Anna Satorie Burich) photo archives provides validity of this story. That's because the newly minted John A. Burich and remaining John J. Burich went down to the local photo studio and posed for a photo. Each wanted to share the news that the John J. Burich issue had been resolved, so the two men ordered postcards after that photo session.

The back of the postcard reads, "Meet Black John J. Burich (standing) and Red John A. Burich (seated). Please update all mailing ledgers so letters get to the right man."

The entangled John Burich issue was resolved by just one letter—A as in Albert.

# 11

# JOHNNY APPLESEED SHIPPED BY TRAIN

Dad sent apples in whiskey barrels to his sister in Crandon," my grandmother Julia, daughter of John and Anna Burich, once confided in me.

With that single seed of insight, and strong trust in my grandmother's memory, I set out in an attempt to determine what became of her aunt Anna (Burich) Schimek and Anna's husband, Emil Schimek.

Could it be true that John "Johnny Appleseed" Burich really sent apples from the farm's orchard to Wisconsin's Northwoods from Reedsville's railroad depot?

Could I finally find the story about John Burich's sister Anna?

If I could fill in the blanks to this missing story, it would account for four of the six children born to Albert and Josephina Burich.

In April 2018, I intensified my search for Anna Burich. It was a deep data dive that took all my accrued talents as a then twenty-three-year-career journalist and amateur genealogist. That's when I stumbled upon the name Elmyra (Schimek) Hobbs of Crandon, Wisconsin.

To say the least, Elmyra is a unique first name, and it matched some postcards I found in our family's archives that were postmarked from Crandon in the early 1900s.

With more fact checking, I confirmed that Elmyra was the youngest of five children born to Anna and Emil Schimek. Yes, the former Anna Burich. And it's from this point that the story about Anna blossomed like John's apple trees in the early spring sun.

*Left*: Anna (Burich) Schimek and her youngest daughter, Elmyra, are shown on a winter day in Crandon. As an adult, Elmyra (Schimek) Hobbs would become president of the Crandon Telephone Company.
*Charles Wilbur.*

*Below*: Anna and Emil Schimek are buried in the Crandon Lakeside Cemetery. Anna Schimek was the great-aunt to Rosalie Geiger (*center left*) and Annette Krueger (*right*). Rosalie is with son Corey Geiger, and Annette is with husband Robert Krueger.
*Author's collection.*

## POSTCARD ANNOUNCED APPLES

As it turns out, Johnny Appleseed, also known as John Burich, would send a postcard to his sister Anna alerting her of the exact day that the apples would be placed on the evening northbound train from Reedsville—the 153 Chicago Northwestern to be exact. That northbound Chicago Northwestern would stop in Reedsville at 5:45 p.m. and make its way to the next stop—Brillion—at 5:57 p.m.

After that it made stops in Forest Junction, Dundas, Kaukauna, Combined Locks, Kimberly and Appleton before it arrived for a major stop at Appleton Junction. The iron horse rolled into that railroad junction or crossroads at 7:10 p.m., according to the 1928 Chicago Northwestern book that listed fifty-four pages of tables for every rail route for the railroad company. That even included service to Los Angeles, San Francisco and Seattle.

By 11:00 p.m., that train would stop near a railroad depot in Crandon.

Johnny's apples were delivered.

Anna and Emil picked those apples up in the morning since the train arrived too late in the evening.

## NORTHWOODS OPENED UP LATER

Now, Reedsville had had a train and passenger service since 1872. However, Wisconsin's Northwoods, in particular Crandon, did not get train service until 1906. Once it opened, however, the railway quickly became a highway, shipping an equal number of both goods and people northbound as it did southbound.

For the fourteen months ending March 1, 1912, an average of 1,212 tickets and cash fares per month were sold at Brillion and an average of 914 per month at Reedsville. That yielded an average monthly revenue of $570.59 and $403.13, respectively, from the two communities.

During 1911, 48 percent of the passengers from Reedsville headed northbound while 42 percent of the Brillion passengers headed the same direction, according to records published in the 1912 edition of the *Railroad Commission of Wisconsin*. This confirms that once the Wisconsin Northwoods was opened up to railroad traffic, people quickly followed, pursuing careers as lumberjacks, farmers and business owners.

On one occasion, Anna and John Burich (*standing far left*) took the train from Reedsville to Crandon to personally deliver apples. Joining them that day were Lizzie and Frank Kirch. The shortest lady standing is Anna (Burich) Schimek. *Charles Wilbur.*

For many immigrants with large families, older children would set out with the hopes of securing an income. The story was replaying just as immigrants had landed from Europe a generation earlier. In some cases, this new railroad route offered a second chance for immigrants to strike it big as homesteaders and business owners.

## BOHEMIA, TO ILLINOIS, TO WISCONSIN

Emil Schimek was born in Prague, Bohemia, on May 19, 1875, and he and his parents, Albert and Catherine (Miks), and siblings, Godfrey, Albert, Louis and Mary, made their way to America.

After spending a year in Chicago, the Schimeks moved to the Reedsville area, where they homesteaded on a forty-acre parcel directly east of the Burich Homestead and directly north of the Satorie Farm. One of the main reasons the Schimek family likely settled in Reedsville is the area had a large Bohemian-speaking population.

Fast-forward to today: our family now owns a portion of the Schimek homestead.

It's an area that relatives always called "Schimekova's Forty," giving the property the full respect of its Bohemian roots. Later, Joe Jerabek would buy the Schimekova homestead. Eventually, a portion of the site, including remains of the Schimekovas' pioneer home, was acquired by the fifth generation to farm in the Burich family.

From that little cabin, the seventeen-year-old Emil could walk across twenty acres due west, a distance of a quarter mile, to court a young Anna Burich. Anna was born on October 16, 1876, on the Burich Reedsville-based homestead about nine years after her parents, Albert and Josephine (Turensky) Burich, came to America from Bohemia.

For Catholic Bohemians, Anna was an extremely popular and desirable name as that also was the name of the mother of Mary, who gave birth to the Christ child. As a result, John "Appleseed" Burich not only had a sister named Anna but his wife also bore the name Anna.

Anna and Emil eventually were married at St. Mary's Church in Reedsville on January 19, 1896. The couple remained in the Reedsville area for a few years, as baptismal records show that a daughter, Emm,a was born in 1896, son Joseph in 1898 and son Paul in 1900.

Between 1900 and 1902, Emil and Anna decided to seek opportunity in Crandon. That's because daughter Elizabeth "Betty" was born in 1902. Anna and Emil named their fourth child for Anna's sister Elizabeth "Lizzie" Burich, who set up John Burich and Anna Satorie on their first date.

# THE LURE

Making a trip to Crandon yielded a great deal of history about our family. It also opened a story about migration from Reedsville to Crandon.

Crandon was flush with opportunity.

Wisconsin's Forest County community leaders, mainly lumber barons and railroad tycoons, were heavily recruiting workers. A large contingent of Kentucky natives traveled north to work in Crandon. As a result, the community's library maintains Blue Grass State genealogy records due to the heavy influx of Kentucky folk.

The recruiting efforts were a mix of truth and tales as tall as Paul Bunyan and Babe the Blue Ox of mythical folklore. The following excerpt from

The Schimek family once owned a farm next to the Buriches. In those days, Emil Schimek and his mother, Catherine (Miks) Schimek, lived just a forty-acre parcel away. Emil's daughter Emma (Schimek) is pictured here holding her son Ronald. *Charles Wilbur.*

the 1914 booklet *Forest County: Where One Potato Crop Buys the Land* details the recruitment efforts. The booklet was published by authority of the County Board of Supervisors, Forest County.

> *Our cut-over lands are not devoid of timber, just the large trees being cut off. Many small trees are still standing, which will help the new settler get started. There is a ready market for wood products, including poplar, basswood, and cedar bolts, ties, poles, posts, pulp-wood, and cord wood. In fact, everything can be sold.*
>
> *These lands can be bought for $10 to $18 per acre, with the terms arranged so that the settler can make a small payment down and have*

*something left for clearing and starting the farm. After he has a few acres cleared and into potatoes, a good living is assured while he clears the remainder of the land.*

*The fame of our clean white Rurals (potatoes) is fast spreading. We get heavy yields on our new soil. Yields of 200 to 300 bushels per acre are common, and the average farm price for the past nine years has been 45 cents per bushel. This leaves a fine profit for the grower.*

*Good, well-improved land is held for as high as $75 per acre and is still going higher as settlement progresses. Forest County is truly the land of opportunity for the man of small means.*

And so they came, including Anna and Emil Schimek from Reedsville, Wisconsin. For Emil, it was his fourth home. He had lived in Prague, Bohemia; Chicago, Illinois; Reedsville, Wisconsin; and now Crandon.

# 12

# THE HOMESTEAD HOUSE HAS GOT TO GO

L og cabins and pine-sided pioneer homes dotted the rural countryside a century ago. Everyone lived in one. The homes were far from plush, but it's all the families could afford.

During summer, family members sweltered in those primitive homes due to the excessive heat. In winter, the wind whistled through cracks in the window sashes and crevices in the logs or clapboard siding. It was downright cold, even with the hottest fire roaring in the woodstove, as those homes had little to no insulation.

On top of all that, one had to scurry outside to use the outhouse, as those pioneer homes had no indoor plumbing. And of course, there was no electricity.

## EIGHT IS ENOUGH

By 1913, John and Anna Burich had been married seven years. Anna had given birth to five children: three daughters were living in the home, but two infant sons died shortly after birth.

A family of five may not sound all that bad. But there were many more. There were actually eight people, five of whom were adults. That was simply too many residents under one roof.

John's father, Albert Burich, now in his mid-seventies, was living with the couple per terms of the farm's purchase agreement. So was Anna's father, Wencel, during the winter months. John and Anna had agreed to that arrangement as part of the contract to purchase Wencel's forty-acre homestead. Then there was John's brother Louis, who couldn't fully care for himself, although he could help with some basic jobs.

So, added to that family of five there were three additional adult men: Albert, Wencel and Louis.

Eight people in one rickety homestead house, with its pine-sided front and log cabin rear, created tension among the family given its close living quarters. There could easily be eleven people living there had Anna and John's two sons lived after birth.

John and Anna wanted a larger home. How could they afford to build it? Just work harder and use available resources—that was John's solution.

## THE THREE-YEAR PROJECT

Gravel. Check.

By 1913, John had established two gravel pits on his property. This supplemented income from the twenty-four-cow dairy herd that the Burich family was milking by hand twice each day.

If John started digging extra gravel and hauling it to the farmstead, he could have the gravel necessary to provide a foundation concrete basement floor for a modern house. The ambitious man in his mid-thirties hauled gravel for two years and eventually separated the rock from the sand, with a screening system to make concrete blocks. That surely would take care of the whistling wind John had grown to despise in his current home.

Lumber. Check.

John and his wife also amassed well over fifty acres of woods that consisted of white and red oak, sugar maple and white pine. With his family to help cut trees, they could take the logs to John's first cousin Louis Turensky, who owned a sawmill.

He would need pine for the wall studs, roof work and wood lath for walls to eventually hold plaster. The maple would become hardwood floors throughout the house, and the oak made splendid doors, cabinets and interior trim.

However, John needed to get started in 1913 because he had to let the wood cure so he could forgo the expense of a kiln to dry the lumber.

"They built this house, which took an awful lot of lumber out of our woods, and gravel from our own pit. Work!!!" wrote John and Anna's daughter Julia years later in a journal entry recalling the events that took place to build that home.

A building plan. Check.

John and Anna wanted everyone to have their own bedroom, so this house was going to be large enough for everyone. The first floor would have a living room, a dining room and a country kitchen large enough to cook for any farm work crew. That first floor also had two bedrooms.

The second floor had two master bedrooms, along with three additional bedrooms. A sixth room would have a modern-day bathroom with water provided by a cistern that collected rainwater from the roof. Gravity would move the water to the bathroom.

The basement was just as grand in size, at least when it came to the walls. Three-foot-thick walls supported the entire structure. John's plan also included a second cistern dug under the basement floor to store additional rainwater.

That overbuilt basement would have five rooms of its own, one of which was to process livestock—as butchering was mainly done on the farmstead, too, in those days. As for the attic, John and Anna clearly were prepared in the event more bedroom space was needed. A full stairwell was created with plans for four additional bedrooms.

While those rooms were never completed, the stairwell was plastered and four dormers were added at ninety-degree intervals in the roof. The house eventually climbed so high that one could see clear to the nearby village of Reedsville or the city of Brillion depending on which dormer one looked out.

The house may have been overbuilt based on its concrete and timber, but it survived a tornado just eight years after its construction that wiped out nearby neighborhood homes and barns. The tornado of 1922 blasted out every glass window on the north side of their new home, but the concrete-block house otherwise stood firm.

As a five-year-old, John and Anna's youngest daughter, Julia, recalled peering out the window and watching the tornado take barns and homes to the north. That window viewing abruptly ended when her father, John, quickly grabbed his curious daughter and hastily fled to the basement for shelter.

## BUILDING COMMENCED IN 1916

After John gathered supplies for three years, they made concrete blocks onsite starting in the spring of 1916. The crew came each morning to mix Portland concrete and fill the forms. Each block had a hollow center. That air space provided additional insulation—remember, John had enough of the winter cold. These special forms created a molded concrete stone-face block.

Why was that molding so important? It allowed the concrete blocks to have a decorative face so the homeowner would not have to paint the house. At the start of each day, the masonry crew would take the forms off the concrete blocks poured just a day earlier and start the process of making new ones. Then they would take the cured bricks and set them in place. One block at a time, the rows began to climb and the house began taking form.

Eventually, the new construction started peering over the fifty-year-old rickety pioneer house that stood to the west, closer to the road. John and Anna's new home was taking form, and the neighbors were starting to take notice.

The following is a recollection from John and Anna's youngest daughter, Julia.

"Albert Prochnow and his masonry crew made the bricks right on the farm," said Julia. "I know because my Uncle Louis helped make them. Louis was my dad's brother, Louis Burich. He lived with us. He was Pa's brother; we had to take care of him. That is what you did in those days.

"Uncle Frank also helped out. He was a well driller," she went on. "He drilled the well in front of the house. After the house was built, he lived with us for a bit longer. Frank eventually got married and moved up north near Crandon."

## MA DID HER PART

"Think of the meals Ma had to prepare for the carpenters, masoners, and farmers helping with the buildings," Julia wrote, recalling narratives from her mother, Anna.

"In those days, builders and work crews ate on the farms," Julia wrote in 1951, about thirty years after the house construction project. "And it was true 'country cooking.'

"I didn't feed the carpenters that built our new shed in 1950, but I fed the farmers when they roofed it. I also fed the plumbers when they put in our new bathrooms along with threshing crews for eight years. In addition, farm wives like my Ma prepared meals when crews came over to saw wood, butchering, and filling silo," continued Julia.

## Only the Best Wood

John used the best wood he could find. Most of that came from the family's woods. Every room had hardwood maple floors. All the doors and trim were made of red oak. The roof joists were made of two-inch-thick-by-eight-inch-wide pine plank.

There was no skimping.

John had a deep disdain for fixing windows and the whistling wind. To that end, Albert Prochnow mentioned to John that California redwood lumber does not rot.

"That's for me!" John must have thought.

So he ordered more than enough to make every window and window frame. All that wood arrived at Reedsville's train depot. John would never fix windows again, except when the tornado blew through.

Sound like a far-fetched story?

Almost a century later, John's granddaughter Rosalie Geiger, the fifth generation on the family farm, was having some repair work done in the house and hired Kenny Mack. The last job she asked Kenny to do was replace a window in the kitchen.

After some investigation, Kenny said, "I can't replace that window frame, Rosie. I think that's made of redwood. It's in pristine condition. Who would have put redwood in this house?"

"That would have been my grandfather," Rosalie said with a grin.

"I'll just replace the glass pane, then, as the rest is in great shape," replied Kenny.

## The First with Electricity

The Delco Light electric plant hit the market in 1916 as the house was going up. This sounded like a swell addition to John for his new home. While nearby Reedsville had electricity since 1906, if you lived in the country you still lived without power.

What was a Delco Light electric plant? In 1916, Charles Kettering founded the Domestic Engineering Company and introduced the Delco Light electric plant to bring electricity to rural America. Joining with battery and appliance manufacturers, Delco Light offered a complete electric power system for flameless lighting, running water and convenient labor-saving equipment and appliances. That running water brought the basement cistern to life.

It was a tremendous success, and General Motors acquired Kettering's company two years later, with Kettering himself heading up research for General Motors. By the late 1920s, sales for Delco Lights would surpass 325,000 units annually.

However, that all changed a few decades later when the Rural Electrification Act of 1936 was signed into law by President Roosevelt. That act brought electricity to all of rural America. Within two years, 100,000 miles of power lines were set into place, delivering electricity to some 220,000 farms.

## TEN AND THEN ELEVEN

Before the house on this hill was completed in late 1916, the Burich family had added a fourth daughter, Beatrice "Bessy" Burich, who would later marry Quiren Sleger. Youngest daughter Julia joined the family on October

John Burich spent three years gathering materials for his house on the hill. Years later, local historians would call the Burich home a "Rusticated Stone Colonial Revival–Period Farmhouse." *Author's collection.*

31, 1918, and was the only child born in the new house. Julia must have been a difficult birth like her brothers, as she was hastily baptized the very next day by Father Kolar.

As for John Burich's grand house on the hill…

In 1980, the Rockland Township listed twenty-seven unique historical building sites in the township. A number of them have since been razed, but number seven on the detailed document still stands as the "Rusticated Stone Colonial Revival–Period Farmhouse."

That's the house that John and Anna built.

# 13

# NO FISH. NO FUNERAL.

At day's end, the two grown men left in dead silence. That's not the way the day started, though, as boisterous banter had previously filled the air.

However, had you witnessed them at that exact moment, you would have surely thought the men had just returned from laying a dear friend to his final rest following a funeral.

The only indication that wasn't the case is those two Americans of full-blooded Bohemian heritage were wide-eyed—flashing eyes nearly bugging out of their heads with fear.

As it turns out, that fear was knowing their own funerals were nearly set into motion.

## SUNDAY FUNDAY

America's pioneers were hardworking folks.

Sunup to sundown, six days a week—that was the work routine for most Wisconsin dairy farmers. In winter, farm folks milked cows by hand with flickering kerosene lanterns providing the light. By the time Sunday came along, morning milking took place mighty early. Then everyone bathed, if they hadn't already done so the night before, and dressed in their Sunday-best clothes before heading off to church. For John, Anna and their family, their congregation was at St. Mary's in nearby Reedsville.

John was an early owner of a Ford Model T, the family's first motor car.

He'd pack wife Anna, their five daughters and his brother Louis into the car and hustle down the road to church. Once church was over, the boys often stopped by nearby Kabat's Brothers Tavern and Harness Repair, while the women and children remained at church for some additional post-service prayer and socializing.

Not only did the beer flow at the tavern, but the trio of Kabat brothers also specialized in leather work for horse harnesses and shoe repair. Get a little work done for the farm and fill up a growler of beer for the trip home. Word had it that Red John was a frequent customer on Sundays, as were many of his Catholic friends.

It's likely at the bar that Red John asked nearby neighbor "Black" John Burich, "Do you want to go fishing today?"

Black John jumped at the chance to be outdoors for a more relaxing endeavor than his normal farm chores. Plus, the fresh catch would be welcomed by the entire family.

On that sunny winter day, the Burich men didn't even have to rent a boat from nearby farmer William Kanter because the duo could drive the Model T right onto the lake due to the winter's ice cover. That notion was like fine polka music ringing right into the ears of these penny-pinching farmers of Bohemian stock.

So each man took his family home and quickly assembled his fishing gear.

When Red John Burich pulled into Black John Burich's yard, the two men were yucking it up as Red John drove the two farmers turned fishermen for the day trip. The lightened mood was enhanced thanks to some fermented suds acquired from Kabat's earlier that day.

Their destination?

Nearby Long Lake. It was one of four area lakes an easy drive from their respective homesteads.


## THE SHORTEST TRIP EVER

As the Burich boys approached Long Lake, Red John turned down a narrow gravel road. They traveled a distance of 80 rods—farmer talk for the length of a 40-acre parcel. A rod was a measuring standard in those days as surveyors marched west across the American frontier creating land deeds: 80 in a length of a 40-acre parcel, 320 rods to a section of 360 acres. Those 320 rods were exactly a mile. In those days, roads seldom bore names and mile measurements weren't really needed, as horse and oxen power still fueled the majority of the nation's countryside.

So all the farmers spoke rod, not mile markers.

At that point, Red John drove his 1,200-pound shiny black Model T directly onto Long Lake's ice. With two men and fishing gear, the total weight of the Model T that day likely pushed 1,600 pounds. Red John drove farther onto the lake, heading for their favorite fishing hole.

He knew the lake well.

"That's when Red John flung open the door and quickly grabbed his hatchet. He flung that hatchet with the full strength of a pioneer farmer and it landed on the spot where Red John had anticipated cutting the first fishing hole to drop a line," recalled

After tossing an axe and seeing it fly through the ice, John Burich surely feared for his life that winter day. After careful maneuvering, John and his friend were able to get the Model T off of Long Lake. *Author's collection.*

Bernard "Barney" Dvorachek in a story retold to him by his father, Joe J. Dvorachek.

"Splash!"

"The hatchet was gone!"

"Flew right through the ice," said Barney.

"Red John just stared at Black John," Barney added, and "neither uttered a word. Silence filled the cold winter air with the knowledge of the danger that disappearing axe told.

"After making a few hand motions to each other, the men slowly crept towards the car." Barney heard the story multiple times as a child, as he grew up less than a mile from the two Burich families. No doubt Red John and Black John retold the account to their Bohemian brothers after surviving the ordeal and living to tell about it.

"Red John opened the door to the Model T and slowly pushed down the middle of three foot pedals with his hand. And standing outside the car, the 'R' pedal hit the floorboard and the Model T slowly crept backward," related Barney slowing his speech as if the story happened just yesterday.

"Each man carefully ushered that car off the lake," he continued, noting their eyes were pulled wide open like roller blinds to allow dawn's early sun rays through a house window.

"That was the end of the fishing trip! Red John dropped off Black John at his farm," concluded Barney.

"Then Red John drove home to his farm."

No fish.

No funeral.

# 14

# He Drove for Gangsters

Prohibition made people rich, and it made people dead. Both may have applied to Uncle Tom.

"My Pa had three brothers," recalled Julia (Burich) Pritzl. "Frank was a well driller. Louis lived with us and worked as a farmhand. Then there was the well-dressed, dashing ladies' man, Uncle Tom, who was youngest in the family."

"The last time I ever saw Tom was when he came to our home farm in Reedsville." Julia remembered seeing her uncle as she peered out the house window as a five-year-old girl in 1923. "He had one fancy maroon-colored car.

"It was a big, long Buick." Julia went on, "It had a tire on the side of the fender door," noting that she along with her four sisters were instructed to stay in the house as her Pa, John Burich, went out to meet his brother. However, staying in the house didn't stop the five girls—Mary, Agnes, Cecilia, Beatrice and Julia—from peering through the southern windows of their home that faced the family's cow barn. The girls wanted to witness the action.

"Pa was so worried 'they' would find Tom," Julia went on to say, reflecting on the events, not providing much initial detail about the "they" in the story. "So Pa and Tom hid the shiny maroon Buick upstairs in the old cow barn," she recalled, noting it was a type of car no one in the greater Reedsville area had ever seen or driven up until that point.

"Somebody must have been chasing him," she surmised. "Once safely in the second story of the barn, Pa slid the doors closed and braced them shut. Then Pa and Uncle Tom hustled into the house, dimmed the lights and had an unusually quiet dinner by our family's standards.

"Pa was edgy the entire evening. You could just sense it. Tom didn't talk much either," said Julia, who was youngest of five girls in the family. "It was all small talk amongst the adults. When one of us asked a question, it became abundantly clear we were not to be involved in the conversation and the girls were sent to bed early that evening. That was that." Julia knew her place as the family's youngest child.

"My older sisters knew Uncle Tom quite well because he once lived with us. But he was long gone by the time I was born," said Julia. "Given my older sisters long-spoken respect for Uncle Tom, I couldn't figure out why everything was top secret."

Julia wanted to unravel the mystery. She was the only sister bold enough—more likely naïve enough—to do it.

As a young girl, Julia Burich peered in the barn to see Uncle Tom Burich's shiny maroon Buick hidden inside. Her father, John, admonished Julia and told her to stay out. *Author's collection.*

The next day, Julia was sneaking around and went into the barn to get a closer look at the car. Her father found her and sternly said, "Don't come back in the barn, Julia!" He proceeded to cover the car with loose hay. In fact, he literally buried that car in hay.

Julia recalled the events vividly. That would be Uncle Tom's last evening on the farm, as John felt his family was being placed in harm's way.

"Very early the next morning, Tom left." The girls woke early to watch the unfolding saga.

"Before he left, Pa walked out to the barn and helped Uncle Tom pull the hay away from the car.

"Then Pa handed him a gunnysack," said Julia. "I knew it was filled with food because Ma had been feverishly cooking that morning and filled it herself.

"Then Uncle Tom got in the car and drove down our long gravel driveway. Pa stood and watched as the rest of the family remained in the house.

"We never saw Uncle Tom again," she said.

## Uncle Tom Is "Dead"

"Pa came in the house and was very serious. He called everyone to the dining room table and had us five girls sit down," said Julia.

"Strycek Tom de mrtvy!" Pa said in his native Bohemian.

As the oldest daughter started to ask a question, Pa repeated his statement, but this time in English, not Bohemian. In either case, it was just as stern.

"Uncle Tom is dead!"

"But Pa, he just ate breakfast with us," interjected a confused five-year-old Julia.

"He's dead. We had a funeral. He's buried!" John Burich roared back, having just walked into the family's farmhouse and knowing full well that his five curious daughters were watching the early morning events through the window.

"Remember those three lines, in that order," he thundered as he stared down his five daughters. Wife Anna fully backed him up with arms crossed as she stood near the dining room table with a piercing glare to drill the message into each respective daughter's little Bohemian head.

Julia was mightily confused. However, when she glanced over and absorbed the frightened looks on the faces of her four older sisters, she was convinced this was not the time for any more questions.

"He's dead. No more questions!" Pa Burich blurted out once again to put the issue to its final rest.

"For years, our family never uttered the name of Tom Burich in our home," said Julia, who only timidly answered questions on the subject far later in adulthood and only after her parents were both deceased for decades.

## The Prohibition Was Big Money

By 1933, the bootlegging era had come to a close. Congress and the newly elected President Franklin Roosevelt signed legislation that repealed the Eighteenth Amendment established in 1920 prohibiting the sale of alcohol. It ended one of the deadliest times in U.S. history, when gangsters developed elaborate networks to peddle beer, distilled spirits and moonshine.

Northeast Wisconsin, with its strong German heritage, was a supply hub for the Chicago mobsters. Many of the area's Germans hailed from Bavaria, the country's southernmost province. Its neighbor due east was Bohemia.

Tom Burich wasn't running from the law; he was running from fellow gangsters. Given the risk to his family, John Burich declared his brother "dead and buried." *Author's collection.*

To this very day, the people of the Czech Republic, which contains the former Bohemia, rank as the world's biggest beer drinkers. Germany's Bavaria region stands right behind them. That explains a great deal about Wisconsin's beer making and beer drinking traditions. The Badger State once had more bars and taverns than grocery stores, making it truly unique among the fifty U.S. states, according to the authors of *Bottoms Up: A Toast to Wisconsin's Historic Bars & Breweries*.

"Prost!" the German and Bohemians would say before enjoying a fresh lager. Prohibition would not stop that toast.

Most in Northeast Wisconsin strongly believed that Prohibition was anti-immigrant, anti-German, anti-Irish, anti-Lutheran and anti-Catholic.

By the time this period came to a close, Julia had become more enlightened about Tom's profession.

"Tom drove a car for the gangsters in Chicago," Julia continued. "That was during Prohibition when alcohol was illegal."

Guys like Tom were valuable to the gangsters because he knew the country roads and could work with farmers and cheesemakers willing to take the risk of brewing beer or distilling alcohol. Most of the trade was in distilled spirits; more punch could be packed into smaller bottles.

What became of Tom Burich?

While Tom was in church records and census data prior to 1920, he cannot be found in any records thereafter. Born on November 15, 1886, Thomas Burich became a ghost. He was gone in the wind.

He may be at the bottom of a lake, buried in concrete, or maybe he fled under an alias.

But one thing is for sure, after twenty years of intensive research on a Burich family tree: Tom Burich went off the grid for good.

## THE COPPER COW

If your family were bootleggers, the chances are high that you may not even know to this day. That's because many of those family members took the secrets to their grave. Men like Uncle Tom did not want to bring a prison sentence or early death to their unknowing family members.

Everything was kept top-secret. It was a cash-only business. Bootleggers didn't tell their own family members they were in the business for fear of federal agents or, worse, rival gangsters.

When interviewed by John Jenkins for his thesis at Marian University, Victor Sippel of Mount Calvary, Wisconsin, estimated that one out of ten people he knew in the Holyland region east of Wisconsin's Lake Winnebago and west of Lake Michigan was involved in the business of moonshine or distilled spirits.

When yours truly was growing up, I remember hearing some old-timers say the "most profitable cow was the copper cow."

The first time I heard that statement, I didn't understand it. But one old-timer from northeast Manitowoc County shared that the cows were the front to keep a legitimate business. But it was the copper cow—the still—that made the money. Plus, cows could eat the evidence—corn mash or brewers' grain—after the booze was sold.

Most of the work went on late at night. Barns that were used for distilling often had few windows or those windows were completely covered in some way. As extra precaution in Wisconsin's Holyland region, young boys would serve as lookouts manning ropes that went back to the barn. At the end of the rope was a bell. If it rang, the crew in the barn knew trouble was near.

While some cops and federal agents were avidly looking for bootleggers, others looked the other way in return for cash or, better yet, some moonshine or whiskey of their own during the parched Prohibition.

Part of the distilling operation involved sugar. Large quantities were needed to ferment alcohol. And sugar movement was a tipoff to police and rival bootleggers alike. A great deal of sugar transportation took place under cover of the night.

Of course, the other ingredients—corn, barley and other grains—were conveniently on the farm.

## Kasson's Best Still

During Prohibition, "brown bagging" became popular, as adults would drink their favorite liquor from brown paper bags as a way to hide the fact that they were consuming alcohol. My guess is that many folks knew exactly what was going on.

Of the brown baggers in the nearby Kasson area who are now long gone, time and time again it was shared with a young Randy Geiger that Elmer Wolfmeyer had the best "copper cow" in the neighborhood. That became a topic of conversation because my father, Randy Geiger, took ownership of Wolfmeyer's farm.

Randy tried many times to find that still. But Wolfmeyer clearly didn't want it found and took those secrets to his grave upon his death in 1964.

In the early 1970s, a prominent Brillion business owner who drank from the acclaimed "best copper cow" in the area stopped by to help Randy in his search for the famed still. He wanted another sip of that still's sweet nectar.

While the still could not be found after repeated efforts, Randy and his wife, Rosalie, believed the business owner's story. That's because there were well over a dozen bushel baskets of empty whiskey bottles scattered in sheds when the couple acquired the property. So many bottles, the story must have had some merit. And reflecting on that situation, the businessman in question may have helped Wolfmeyer with supplies.

Then there were the three additional facts.

1. By all accounts, Wolfmeyer wasn't a very good farmer.
2. Wolfmeyer was a man of purebred German ancestry. He always seemed to have green money despite his less-than-thrifty farm.
3. Wolfmeyer also had a milk route delivering bottled milk door-to-door. That legitimate business gave the perfect cloak for bootlegging whiskey.

Years later, Randy's younger brother, Albert, purchased the property. At that point, the legendary whiskey-making cauldron still hadn't given up its location.

Eventually, Albert and his wife, Kay Lynn, built a new home. That construction project resulted in two things: tearing down an old shed and the old farmhouse.

## LEGENDS SELDOM DIE

The high hoe operator hired that day took his time tearing down that shed—carefully as if a skilled surgeon performing heart surgery. He, too, was a Kasson boy and knew about the legend of that still and likely drank its whiskey at one point.

When the high hoe's arm found copper coils, the destruction ceased. The still was hidden in an elaborate false floor in the granary.

There were murmurs in the Kasson neighborhood that Wolfmeyer's still had been found. While the prominent Brillion business owner who searched with Randy never lived to see the still again, a local farmer clearly knew it existed.

"Was it empty?" asked Clarence Tesch with a big grin on this face.

Clarence was serious. He wanted one last drink.

The still found in the shed remains in the family's possession as a reminder of a bygone era of bootleggers, gangsters and copper cows.

The only question that remains is where was Uncle Tom's bootlegger booty?

# 15

# THE BOOTLEGGERS' BOOTY

Tom Burich was a dashing man. That exact word—*dashing*—was inscribed on the flipside of one of the family photos that included Tom Burich. For decades, those photos lay buried deep at the bottom of a box of family heirlooms.

While Tom may have been a short fellow, he had the looks that turned women's heads. Dark curly hair, brown eyes—above all, Tom was an extremely sharp dresser. He was simply handsome.

In one classic 1920s photo, Tom is sporting a new suit, and in the same photo, his older sister Elizabeth is wearing a fancy mink coat and hat. Elizabeth's adornments were compliments of younger brother Tom.

He looked like a gangster and spent money like one, too. Oh yes, Tom had money—apparently lots of it.

Crisp bills—as in cold hard cash. That left a mystery to unravel.

From 1920 to 1923, Tom had routinely been making round trips from somewhere in rural Reedsville to Chicagoland. Where was Tom's bootlegger booty? Where was Tom's supply depot?

I asked those questions out loud while drinking some chokecherry wine one evening during Wisconsin's 2018 gun deer hunt. The question was rather apropos given that wine came from a homemade batch fermented by neighbor Scott.

"Henry's farm," said Scott. The other men looked at me, and all nodded in unison as if I were dense or dimwitted.

"Don't know the guy," I retorted.

Donning this new suit, Tom Burich bought his older sister Lizzie a fancy mink coat and hat. Did Tom buy these clothes from profits earned from bootlegging? The answer is likely "Yes." *Author's collection.*

That's when the group of deer hunters began telling me a story. But was the story fact or fiction?

As I listened, my brain leapt straight back to the 1920s, as I had memorized every plat book and farm location in the era for generations. The more they shared insight, my brain's truth or fiction meter trended toward truth based on their testimony.

Scott's home was nestled on a large outcropping the locals referred to as the Rock. Its two-word name held for generations dating far back to the very first homesteaders. To this very day, you can see fireworks over twenty miles away on a clear Fourth of July night from this high limestone outcropping. It stretches in every direction for over a mile with an elevated height of a few hundred feet.

In the 1920s, the trees would have been short after the area had been logged off via the clear-cut method where every tree succumbed to the saw. Later, the entire land area was grazed by farm animals, limiting any trees growing past one's vision.

From this vantage point, a person could have easily seen the farm of John Burich and Henry's farm, too. In fact, both sites would have been equidistant from that vantage point. One of those lookouts on the Rock was owned by Tom's sister-in-law Mrs. John A. Burich in those days. A shrewd Tom could have perched up on that hill and seen traffic for miles.

But did this Henry fella own the farm in question during the 1920s? That answer could be found in a vintage Manitowoc County plat book.

When Bohemians first flocked to the Reedsville area, Frank Burich originally homesteaded that farm.

Frank and his wife, Anna, had a number of children. One happened to be Charles Burich. By 1921, the plat book recording for that farm read, "Chas Burich." Years earlier, it was owned by a Frank Burich.

Arriving from the same hometown in the old country, bootlegger Tom Burich's father, Albert Burich, and Frank Burich—as in the father of Charlie—were brothers. Bootlegger and booty were once again reconnected.

Adding to the story was the fact Julia always said, "Charlie Burich isn't a relative." Why would she claim Charlie wasn't her Pa's first cousin when unearthed obituaries say otherwise?

If your family beats into your head that "Uncle Tom is dead," surely the statement "Charlie Burich isn't our relative" could have been browbeaten into the young Burich girls.

My hunch is the narrative went like this:

*Uncle Tom is dead. Charlie Burich is not our relative.*

Repeat.

*Uncle Tom is dead. Charlie Burich is not our relative.*

There was another connection: Tom's sister Elizabeth—the same one who received a fancy mink coat from Tom—married Frank Kirch.

As it turns out, Frank Burich, the father of Charlie Burich, married a Kirch, too—as in Anna Kirch.

That's an extremely strong double family connection.

That family connection mattered profusely if people were going to become "partners" in a bootlegging business. They needed to get the work done and keep their mouths shut. If mouths didn't stay shut, people died. No one ever talked openly about stills in that day. Only decades later would people murmur about the illegal trade.

## The Booze Flowed Farther North

In fact, it may have been one of the reasons that the Green Bay Packers survived and became a NFL juggernaut. That's because free-flowing beer and distilled spirits continued even through Prohibition.

For starters, Northeast Wisconsin had plenty of unsanctioned liquor. Second, Green Bay's switchboard telephone operators were in on the action, alerting local officials when federal agents were coming to make liquor busts. When federal agents would call from Chicago and Milwaukee to alert locals that agents were coming up to make the bust, the first call went to the police. Able to listen in on the conversations, switchboard operators made additional calls to the bars, and the booze all got moved in plenty of time.

That's according to the *Legacy*, a ten-part series on the Green Bay Packers produced in 2019 and 2020. Because of that free-flowing liquor, Curly Lambeau could more easily recruit talent than his dried-out competitors. Plus, no one needed Al Capone and his gangsters to make the system work. The "Northeast Wisconsin Mafia" of Bavarians, Bohemians and Irish had it all figured out.

## The Booty

After a little digging, one thing became rather clear. That particular farm definitely had all the attributes to distill the bootlegger's booty. Plus it had another interesting factor: far more buildings than necessary for a farm of that size.

While Charles "Charlie" Burich owned the property during Prohibition, it turns out a young boy named Henry Bubolz grew up directly across the road. By 1945, Henry had acquired the property from the Burich family.

Could Henry have learned the stilling craft from the Burich gang? You be the judge.

"The house is interesting," said Dave Bauknecht, who owns the property these days. "There were three to four ways to get out of the house and water lines went in every direction." He added that he found numerous remnants of attributes necessary to run stills—lots of stills.

"Then there was the fact one never left sober when paying a visit," Dave recalled.

"Word had it back in the day there was a built-in cooler," said nearby dairy farmer John Ebert, who alluded to the fact that someone at that location had been "in the business" in previous years. At one time, there reportedly was even a plane that helped deliver the farm's precious distilled cargo.

Henry's daughter Diana did say that her father made moonshine, but "he wouldn't have made enough to sell."

Diana downplayed the notion that Charlie Burich and his wife, Annie, could have been involved in bootlegging. "Not sweet Charlie and Annie," she confided in me.

"The best secrets are those never spoken," I kindly retorted in a phone conversation with Diana. We agreed to disagree.

As for Uncle Tom, the bootleggers' run would have been an easy one as the road leading to Charlie's farm eventually became State Highway 32. A two-mile jaunt to the west after making a pickup at Charlie's and Tom would have been safely back to his brother John's farmstead, located a bit more off the beaten path. And that homestead's long driveway would have offered protection, as would have a back route escape to the Rock via an unmarked trail that to this day can handle a farm truck.

Once through the woods via the trail established by his brother John's and sister-in-law Anna's marriage, Tom could have skedaddled in any direction. He knew all the cow trails and backroads.

With a good night's rest or a quick escape, Tom Burich would be ready for another run to Chicagoland to deliver his bootlegger's booty.

While some may doubt that Charlie Burich had a still, one must remember that mum was definitely the word on those business operations. Then there's the fact the next generation of Reedsville's schoolboys would get more nervous than a teenager asking a girl out for a date when well-dressed men

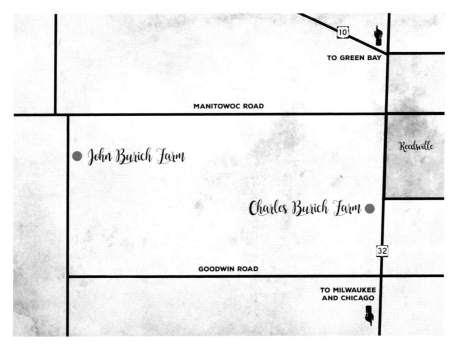

Tom Burich was ferrying alcohol from an undisclosed location in Reedsville to outlets in Chicago. The stills likely were located at cousin Charlie Burich's farm. *C. Todd Garrett.*

driving cars with Illinois license plates pulled over in Reedsville on their way to the Northwoods.

"You scared, kid?" asked one Illinois bar patron when ordering a round from the teenage bartender named Bernard Kubale, who was tending bar in his father's stead.

"Nah, I just want to make sure you get a full shot," said Bernard, who admitted he was flat-out lying to the four patrons in his book *The Place to Meet Your Friends.* Bernard's hands were shaking like leaves on a quaking aspen during the windiest of fall days.

They laughed, and one of the well-dressed men quipped, "Maybe you ought a try one, steady your nerves."

Even though Prohibition was over, local youths were wary of those who had the appearance of a gangster.

One thing's for sure, Tom was obtaining bootlegger's booty from somewhere in the greater Reedsville area.

Only those buried deep in graves can confirm the location of those stills. As for Tom, he has no known grave, as he likely crossed the wrong bootlegger and wouldn't give up his booty.

# 16

# STAY OUT OF THAT CAVE

What do teenage children do when parents issue a warning? Sometimes they heed the advice—in many other instances those words spark adventure and even defiance.

*"Stay out of that cave!"*

That was the command issued by Anna Burich to her daughters Julia and Beattie. Of course, the teenagers' hearing filter transcribed that edict to *"Let's go check it out."*

So Julia and Beattie snuck off, against their mother's wishes, and scurried south from the family farm to the Rock. That limestone outcropping stretched far past their parents' land to property owned by the Schmidt family, who were nearby dairy farmers. Like the Burich family, the Schmidts were one of many second-generation immigrants who owned land in Rockland Township.

"We would shimmy down the opening and play house in that cave," said John and Anna's daughter Julia of her excursions. "We would take gas lanterns so that we could see once we arrived in the cave's main chamber."

"Where is that cave?" asked Julia's curious grandson upon hearing the story.

Just like her mom advised her years earlier, *"Stay out of that cave!"* Julia commanded. "It's filled in with dirt and debris. You might get stuck," she continued.

While Julia never disclosed its location, I didn't venture out to look for it either because I wasn't sure if I believed her. That all changed when I read a newspaper column the summer of 1991 after I graduated from high school.

Teenagers flocked to the Schmidt cave. Among those explorers were the Burich sisters Julia, Agnes and Mary with fellow explorer Agnes (Jerabek) Miller, who lived nearby. *Author's collection.*

## SCHMIDT'S ROCK

"A short time ago, we talked about cave areas in the Maribel Caves region," wrote Syd Herman in his "Sparks from the Campfire" column that appeared in Manitowoc's *Lakeshore Chronicle* in 1991. "Not much new stuff came out of that—maybe because some of the people concerned in my article that were there about 30 or so years ago have since passed away.

"But we did hear about a new one through Elmer Rusch, the historian from Reedsville. He tells about a forgotten cave at what was known as Schmidt's Rock, an outcropping about three miles southwest of Reedsville."

Upon reading this, I wondered if this was the cave Grandma Julia spoke of in earlier stories to me. Elmer Rusch had been the family's longtime neighbor, and I purchased his 1983 Delta 88 Oldsmobile as my first automobile.

## There's Gold in That Rock

"As I heard it, Karl Schmidt, then in his early 20's, lived there in the late 1880s and suspected that the ledge contained minerals—probably gold," wrote Herman.

Schmidt wasn't the only mineral hunter in those days. Dr. Sidney McBride, the only doctor in the Brillion area during the 1870s, owned and investigated the land that eventually became Brillion's lime quarry. McBride hoped the red stone he saw was marble. He purchased the land, built a derrick and opened a twenty-square-foot quarry to test the limestone, hoping to strike it rich.

Not finding what he was looking for, McBride leased the quarry to the Ormsby Lime Company in 1880 for twenty years.

McBride added a stipulation to the lease, claiming all rock below a certain point was his. However, when the company failed to turn up marble of any worth, the doctor sold the land to the lime company before the lease was up, wrote the authors of the book *Brillion Wisconsin 1885 to 2010.*

## Back to Schmidt's Dig

"So he and a few friends dug a 45-degree shaft angling downward about 2-½ feet wide and then leveled out about 15 feet underground where they fashioned a room about 10 feet square from which they intended to run a network of shafts," Herman continued, recounting his in-depth interview with Rusch.

Upon reading this article years later, I wondered how Elmer Rusch could know so much detail about this cave.

After I did a little genealogy work, that answer became crystal clear.

Not only did Elmer farm in the area, but his parents were William and Ida (Schmidt) Rusch. Yes, Ida Schmidt, as in Schmidt's Rock. Ida's father, William Schmidt, was the son of Carl Schmidt. Yes, Carl spelled with a C. Syd Herman spelled his name with a K in the newspaper account.

Carl was born on June 23, 1835. After reading his gravestone, I learned Carl died on March 12, 1887. So that cave was chiseled out of the rock well before 1887, as Carl died at age fifty-two.

"But after finishing the room and finding no minerals, they abandoned the idea," continued Herman. "Today, the shaft is deserted and the entrance hidden by brush and an accumulation of dead leaves. To the best of anybody's knowledge, nobody has been in the underground room in many years."

How accurate was Elmer Rusch's memory? The reader can be the judge of that. However, I witnessed Elmer painting trees deep in the woods to mark property lines solely based on his memory. He and his brother Aron were like coonhounds that could unearth a trail.

Years later, an official surveyor came out to do the same for some property sales in the area. As it turns out, Elmer was only inches off from the professional. Elmer and Aron had only landmarks and trees to guide them in the densely wooded area, not modern-day global positioning system (GPS).

## Let's Go Explore

"Dennis Delaney, a former Reedsville native, said he used to go down there as a boy but the size of the opening is now too small to chance going in again," Herman wrote in that same 1991 article.

"He suggested I go, but I wouldn't fit through the opening either—even if I did, I would hesitate," wrote Herman. "Holes in rock outcroppings and rock caves are often the hibernation site for hundreds of snakes that go below the frost line to spend the winter.

"Anybody else know anything more about the cave? Tell me about it!"

Those were the final words Syd Herman wrote on the topic, as I attentively followed his column for the ensuing weeks. Looking back, I wondered who Dennis Delaney was and why might he have explored those caves.

Dennis grew up in the Reedsville area. His parents, Byron and Edith Delaney, had four children. From 1915 to 1920, Byron was principal of Reedsville High School. Later, he was affiliated with Piepenburg and Reichart Ford Motor Agency from 1920 to 1940. After that, Byron Delaney served as Reedsville's postmaster until 1956. Dennis Delaney's parents were married five years after Julia Burich's parents, John and Anna. Dennis would have explored those caves about the same time as Julia did with her sister Beattie.

## A Popular Hangout

After reading the article, I asked older area residents about the cave. Most had nothing to add. That was until Roman "Buster" Kugle stopped me one day. Buster was a Reedsville legend who was a member of the 1946 State Championship basketball team in the day when all schools competed against one another in the same league. Reedsville had earned its state championship by defeating Eau Claire. The Eau Claire school had more teachers than Reedsville had students at the time. Also on that team was Rueben Rusch, a cousin to Elmer Rusch.

Buster was a legend, and I was all ears.

"I've been down there many times," said Buster.

"What's it like?" I asked.

"We used it as a hangout," said Buster. "It's a room ten feet by ten feet with a six- to seven-foot ceiling."

As our conversation continued, I surmised that Buster and his friends may have been among the last people to be in the cave.

## The Schmidts

The parcel of land where the cave is likely located—and I write "likely" because I haven't yet found its entrance—is a forty-acre parcel once owned by Carl Schmidt and then his son William.

After that, the property was divided between three of the four Schmidt children. Ida (Schmidt) Rusch and her husband, William, took possession of a twenty-acre parcel; Arno received a ten-acre parcel; and John garnered ten acres. All three farmed within a good country holler for a number of decades. A fourth sibling, Hattie (Schmidt) Stebane, lived near Forest Junction.

The knowledge of who had possession of the cave likely died when Elmer Rusch, Ida and William's son, passed away in 2007.

As for me, I heeded my grandmother's advice and stayed out of that cave. But that's only because I could not find it.

# 17

# SHE GAVE HERSELF
# A DEATH SENTENCE

*Death was the victor and it came to relieve her suffering.*

It's rare one reads a statement of that nature in an obituary. However, that's exactly what appeared in the *Manitowoc Pilot* on December 6, 1923, following the death of Alzbeta Kirch.

She was thirty-eight years old.

Alzbeta was the Bohemian name of a woman known to English speakers as Elizabeth. However, all her friends, including her family, simply called her Lizzie. In her younger days, Lizzie was the life of the party and went out of her way to help others. When including the opening statement of this article, those left behind to mourn Lizzie's passing clearly realized that Lizzie was suffering no more even though the tears continued to flow.

## LIVED VIVACIOUSLY

Lizzie played matchmaker, bringing Anna Satorie and John Burich together. In the early 1900s, both Anna and John still being single at age twenty-eight meant they were likely to spend the rest of their lives unmarried. Anna had no time for dating, as she was farming with her widowed father. Meanwhile, John had all he could handle running his 160 acres and caring for his father and brother.

In selecting Frank Kirch as his best man, John Burich reversed the matchmaking tables. Frank later married John's sister Elizabeth "Lizzie" Burich, who was maid of honor at John and Anna Burich's wedding. *Author's collection.*

But Lizzie worked hard to convince her brother to ask Anna out. John's parents pulled him out of school in the second grade, and he didn't think he was smart enough to date Anna. Meanwhile, Anna had her own self-esteem issues; she often pointed out her hands and feet were "as large as any man."

Lizzie would have none of it and worked to make the match. Anna and John married in 1906—with Lizzie as maid of honor and Frank Kirch as the best man. Frank wasn't family—at least not yet.

John Burich had three brothers: Frank, Louis and Thomas. However, he chose Frank Kirch to be his best man. Kirch was roughly the same age as John and also a dairy farmer just one mile due west down the road.

As it turns out, Frank was sweet on John's kid sister, Lizzie, who had just turned twenty when the couple married. As the relationship blossomed between the two, Lizzie became like a big sister to Frank's younger sister Emma, born in May 1893.

It's this friendship that ultimately would cost Lizzie her life.

## EMMA GOT LIZZIE SICK

Tuberculosis is spread through the air when an infected person coughs out infected air droplets from their lungs. As the disease progresses, the coughing becomes more intense as the lungs begin to fill with fluid.

Consumption took Emma Kirch's life on July 28, 1909, at the ever-so-tender age of sixteen. Consumption was the code word for tuberculosis in those days. And Lizzie's helpful nature attending to the sick Emma most undoubtedly caused her to contract the deadly lung bacteria.

Emma's tombstone in St. Mary's Cemetery is befitting the loss of the teenage daughter of Frank and Anna Kirch Sr. An inscription, written in Bohemian, reads as follows in English: "Be with God, oh dear daughter, God has called thee from this valley of tears and given you an eternal home in heaven."

Tuberculosis is a fickle disease. One can die rather quickly from tuberculosis, as was the case with Emma. One can also live with tuberculosis for years, as was the case with the famed gunfighter Doc Holliday, who once rode with Wyatt Earp in the American West.

It was also the case with Lizzie, who contracted tuberculosis and lived with the disease over a decade.

Some would say that Lizzie (Burich) Kirch (*left*) and Emma Kirch were inseparable. However, Emma would soon perish from "consumption," which was another name for tuberculosis. *Author's collection.*

# THE SANATORIUM

Just like Doc Holliday, Lizzie knew the end was near, and she checked herself into the sanatorium in the fall of 1923. Sanatoriums were treatment facilities for the growing number of people infected with tuberculosis.

The Maple Crest Sanatorium, located just north of Whitelaw, was started with a 1910 resolution by the Manitowoc County Board. That year, 50 people in Manitowoc County died of consumption with another 250 reported cases. Young Emma Kirch never made it to the sanatorium, as she died one year prior to its construction.

The first patient was admitted on February 20, 1913, reported Amy Meyer of the *Herald Times Reporter.* By that September, twenty-seven patients had been admitted to the facility—of whom seven died in its first year. The facility even had its own water tower that stood for over a century.

Unfortunately or fortunately—depending on one's perspective and interpretation—Lizzie's stay would be brief.

Those left behind sided with fortunate when writing the line "death was the victor and came to relieve her suffering." The eventual death can be extremely painful because those infected with tuberculosis essentially drown as the lungs fill up with fluid and the body becomes devoid of oxygen. Hence this obituary:

> *The summons of death called Mrs. Frank W. Kirch at the Whitelaw sanatorium last Thursday, where she had been taken three weeks previous with the hope of affording relief from her illness. But death was the victor and came to relieve her suffering.*
>
> *Beside her husband, she is survived by three brothers and one sister.*
>
> *Mrs. Kirch was 38 years of age at the time of her death and was highly esteemed for her kindly disposition and friendly acts.*
>
> *The funeral was held Saturday at the home in Maple Grove with a funeral mass at St. Mary's Church, Reedsville.*

# LOVE ETCHED IN STONE

Frank was still a relatively young man, widowed at age forty-three. Stricken with grief, he purchased a large black granite tombstone that rests in the graveyard across from St. Mary's Church.

Frank Kirch died at age eighty-five knowing a life of loss. Not only did his first wife, Lizzie (*left*), pass away at age thirty-eight, Frank's dear sister Emma (*right*) died at age sixteen. While Frank would remarry Anna Jelinski, she left Frank a widower the final twenty-one years of his life. *Author's collection.*

Adorned with cattails, wheat and daisies, the ornate gravestone shows his love for his fallen wife who sacrificed her very own health in caring for his sister two decades earlier. The tombstone, written in Bohemian, reads:

> *KIRCH*
> *Alzbeta Kirch, manzelka Frantiska Kircha.*
> *Nar. 24 Ledna 1885*
> *Zem. 22 List. 1923*
> *Dopocivej v Pokoji*

The tombstone, when translated to English, reads:

*KIRCH*
*Elizabeth Kirch, husband Frank Kirch.*
*Born January 24, 1885*
*Died November 22, 1923*
*Rest in peace*

Tuberculosis caused Lizzie to die far too young. However, the tuberculin virus would be the first of two virus-borne grim reapers to strike down a Burich family member. Another debilitating and equally deadly disease would strike again in three years.

# 18

# WHITEWASH THOSE BARNS

While Lizzie likely contracted tuberculosis from her sister-in-law, Emma Kirch, tuberculosis was also wreaking havoc in cows. Tuberculosis is a zoonotic disease, meaning it crosses over from animals to humans.

In 1895, former Wisconsin governor W.D. Hoard and editor of *Hoard's Dairyman* began promoting a tuberculosis eradication program. Armed with new insight from leading researchers, the bitter campaign would last forty-five years. Bitter because the struggle cost *Hoard's Dairyman* thousands of canceled subscriptions and lost revenue as the magazine battled almost alone in the early years to free herds from heavy health losses and protect the consuming public from milk-borne tuberculosis. For dairy farmers, the bitter portion would be "destroying" cows that tested positive for tuberculosis. The condemnation was enforced by the law.

It should be remembered that when Hoard began his crusade, America's dairy industry was not unlike dairy sectors that still prevail in many developing countries of the world. On city streets, wagons carried dinged cans of warm milk. A tin dipper was used to fill the housewives' pans and pitchers. Among the millions of multiplying bacteria in milk were *tubercle bacilli*, *Brucella abortus* and many other human health hazards.

Building on the work of German bacteriologist Robert Koch, who had isolated the tuberculosis bacillus, University of Wisconsin scientists developed a test to detect the disease. Farmers were not convinced, so Professor Harry Russell conducted demonstrations at the Wisconsin State Fair. W.D. Hoard heavily promoted the event to drive attendance.

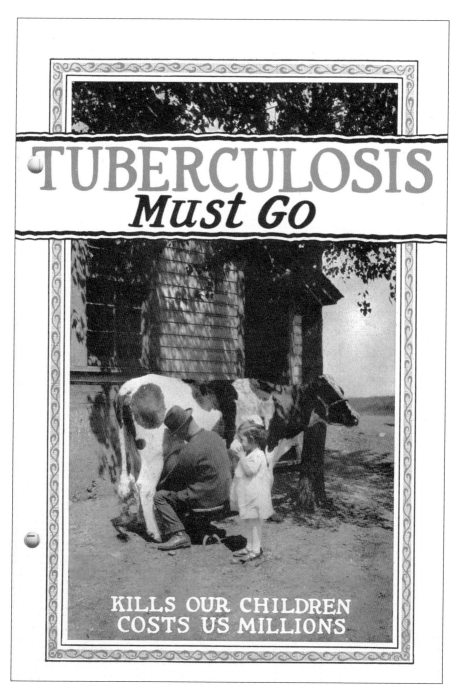

Health regulators waged war against bovine tuberculosis, as the zoonotic disease could cross over and infect humans. *Hoard's Dairyman.*

After seeing the results from the tuberculin test, ten thousand people witnessed the diseased cow lungs as Russell sacrificed the cows at the Wisconsin State Fair park. He showed that the test worked and these cows were already on the way to death from tuberculosis. Similar presentations were done at seven county fairs in Wisconsin. Word started to get out.

This was a big deal because sick cows could pass the disease to humans drinking the milk. Eventually, Russell and E.H. Farrington determined that if milk was pasteurized, or heated up, to 135° to 140° F, the tuberculosis and other bacteria would be killed and the milk safe to drink.

That led Chicago to issue its own milk ordinance around milk sanitation. The debate was so hot that the case went to the Supreme Court. The justices agreed that Chicago's leaders were within their rights to establish public health rules and dairy farmers had to comply in order to sell milk.

After twenty-two years of *Hoard's Dairyman* campaigning for tuberculosis eradication, the federal government finally launched a program in 1917 that led to "cattle testing wars." Now with the full weight of the federal government, tuberculosis-positive herds were immediately condemned. Farmers fought condemnation of tubercular cattle and instead bootlegged

Following the creation of the Pasteurized Milk Ordinance (PMO), milk inspectors verified that whitewash had been applied seasonally inside the milking area. *Author's collection.*

them into untested areas. As the battle ensued, *Hoard's Dairyman* editors courageously addressed mobs of angry farmers throughout the country.

Eventually, sanitation laws also went from city-based propositions to a program run by the federal government. We know those rules as the Pasteurized Milk Ordinance or PMO. Those who milk cows for a living may know this legacy by the fact that state or federal regulators come to evaluate the farm. Those inspectors started coming because of bovine tuberculosis.

While tuberculosis can still infect humans, the final victory against bovine tuberculosis came in 1940 when the entire nation was declared free of bovine tuberculosis. Medical leaders hailed the campaign as "man's greatest victory over tuberculosis."

## DISINFECT THOSE BARNS

Then there's the matter of reducing disease transmission in dairy barns. Of course, that's where farm families milk their dairy cows and gather food for human consumption.

In 1910, former governor W.D. Hoard delivered this message to the Wisconsin Dairyman's Association, the premier dairy trade association of its day. "I note I am to say something to you about this question of tuberculosis. The program says I am to speak from the standpoint of the law," said Hoard, who had just celebrated his fiftieth wedding anniversary that year. "I wish much rather [to] speak from the standpoint of my own experience," recorded the stenographer who always traveled with Hoard.

That "experience" came from his Hoard's Dairyman Farm. As it turns out, Hoard bought four heifers that carried tuberculosis. "I kept on steadily testing every six months and giving my stables thorough disinfection by liberal use of whitewash and other disinfectants," continued Hoard in discussing how he cared for his herd after the tuberculosis outbreak.

## WHITEWASH THOSE BARNS

It's from this basis that whitewashing barns became the norm. While professional services later came to farms to apply the product, that wasn't always the case.

A number of ingredients went into making whitewash. In addition to water, one of the major ingredients was hydrated lime—hence the white color. *Author's collection.*

The Burich family routinely used this whitewash recipe to disinfect their barns:

- Mix 7.5 gallons of water
- 2 pounds of salt
- 10 pounds of hydrated lime
- 4 ounces of powdered alum
- Allow it to soak overnight.
- Special note—for a wood or stone surface, it's advisable to add a pound of glue.

Before that whitewash was applied, the walls needed to be cleaned. Today, whitewash companies often use pressurized air compressors and hoses to remove dust, dirt and debris. Decades ago, that endeavor was a manual process often involving brooms to sweep cobwebs and dirt from ceilings and walls.

Ever frugal farmers, the Burich family and others like them cut branches from cedar trees. Those branches with "leaves" resembling bristle brushes did a wonderful job knocking down cobwebs—just so long as there was a strong-armed operator at the end of those cedar branches.

With the large families of the day, barn cleaning with cedar boughs became just another job like splitting firewood.

# 19

# THREE TERRIBLE CRIES

"Wait up! Wait up! Wait up!"

That shout rang out from one of the five Burich sisters as they walked and at times jogged home from school on a crisp early autumn afternoon with lunch pails and schoolbooks in tow.

However, that shout did not come from Julia, an eight-year-old, the youngest in the family. The plea came from Cecilia, the middle child, who was in the eighth grade at St. Mary's Catholic School. She was just days away from her thirteenth birthday on September 27.

Answering the plea, Julia slowed down as eighteen-year-old Mary, sixteen-year-old Agnes and eleven-year-old Beatrice bounded for home down the two-mile stretch of a gravel township road. It's the daily route they took because there were no school buses. Only occasionally did the sisters get a ride from their parents if it was snowing or raining. And even then, those rides were rare.

"Something is not right with my foot and leg," Cecilia shared with her younger sister. "It's really sore, and I am having trouble moving it."

The two sisters continued home and most certainly shared this development with their parents, John and Anna Burich, later that evening.

## Multiple Family Deaths

Anna lost her firstborn, Wencel Burich, just hours after he entered the world on September 15, 1907. Named after her father, Wencel, the baby's death really set Anna back on her heels.

A rather substantial grave marker, especially for a newborn baby, marks little Václav Burich's final resting place. There is a short message inscribed on the marker:

> *In Bohemian*
> *Nás malý synácek spí sladce zde.*
>
> *In English*
> *Our little son sleeps gently here.*

Picking up the emotional pieces, she trudged on with daily household chores for husband John; his father, Albert; her brother-in-law Louis; and her father, Wencel, who all lived in the family's pioneer house. Lots of men, but no women to comfort Anna and lend emotional support after her son's death.

Mary and Agnes, who were born next, now were attending Reedsville High School.

Adolph, a popular German and Bohemian name for boys prior to the arrival of Adolf Hitler and the outbreak of World War II, was born on June 18, 1912. He lived five days. And once again, Anna was planning a funeral. This time the funeral would be for her last baby boy.

By January 1926, Anna had held four more visitations in her home. Father-in-law Albert Burich died in 1916. Her father, Wencel, passed in 1920, and John's brother Louis died in January 1926. Those were just the people who were living in the family home. Matchmaker Lizzie, John's gregarious sister who brought Anna and John together, died in 1923 from tuberculosis. Her widower, Frank, asked that that visitation service be held in the Burich family home.

By this time, John and Anna had a household of five girls. Cecilia was born in 1913, Beatrice in 1915 and Julia in 1918. Given the parents' collective past experiences with life and death, they took Cecilia's situation very seriously.

A young Cecilia Burich, shown center with older sisters Mary and Agnes flanking her in this 1914 photo. *Author's collection.*

## STRAIGHT TO GREEN BAY

With no improvement during the coming days after visiting Reedsville's local doctor, John headed to Green Bay with Cecilia in the family's black Buick sedan. Anna stayed behind to tend to the four girls and run the farm.

Founded in 1888 by four Catholic nuns who belonged to the Third Order of St. Francis, St. Vincent Hospital had the most-up-to-date X-ray and laboratory equipment. The hospital also had a new surgical wing.

Upon examination, the doctors didn't like what they saw. Physicians told John that Cecilia had "rheumatic trouble." John winced.

He instantly knew that was the code for the dreaded disease polio. The word *rheumatic*, which described diseases that affect joints, tendons, ligaments, bones and muscles, was the term used in those days because polio incited fear. Just years earlier in New York City, the names and addresses of individuals with confirmed polio cases were published in the daily press, their homes were identified with placards and their families were quarantined.

Looking back on the situation, this is clearly the reason that the Health Insurance Portability and Accountability Act (HIPAA) was signed into law in order to protect patient privacy. That wasn't the case in 1926.

"They didn't know much about polio in those days," remembered Julia. "Pa took her to the Green Bay hospital, but they couldn't help her. Cecilia just kept getting worse." By December, Cecilia was no longer going to school, as she was losing control of all her muscles.

Prior to the twentieth century, polio infections mainly occurred in children six months to four years of age. When contracting the viral infection at that young age, children generally suffered only mild symptoms and then developed immunity to the disease.

Modern-day sanitation changes all that. Improved sewage disposal such as indoor toilets and clean water supplies meant infants and children had fewer opportunities to encounter the virus and develop resistance. That meant exposure to poliovirus was delayed until late childhood or adulthood. At that stage of life, polio caused paralysis or death.

## THE LAST CHRISTMAS

There is no doubt the Christmas of 1926 was a somber one. By then, Cecilia's condition had worsened. "It finally took her on December 27," said a teary-eyed Julia recalling the death of her thirteen-year-old big sister. At the time of Cecilia's death, Julia would have been a third grader at St. Mary's grade school.

What follows is an account written by Winifred Meany, the Reedsville representative for Manitowoc's *Herald Times Reporter*, on December 30, 1926:

> *The funeral of Cecilia Burich, thirteen year old daughter of Mr. and Mrs. John A. Burich of Rockland was held from St. Mary's Church at 10*

Taken shortly before contracting polio, Cecilia Burich is shown with younger sister Julia. As her classmates laid Cecilia to her final rest, this is the image of Cecilia that would have been etched into their memory. *Author's collection.*

*o'clock Wednesday morning, Rev. J.W. Decker reading the requiem High Mass and the burial rites at the grave.*

*Deceased was taken ill several months ago with rheumatic trouble and for a time it was hoped she would recover, but for the past month she had grown weaker and on Monday morning she passed quietly away. She leaves to mourn her death, besides her parents, four sisters.*

*She was a pupil at St. Mary's Catholic school and dearly beloved by the Sisters of the school and her classmates, six (boys) of whom were pallbearers at the funeral with eight girls as honorary pallbearers.*

That's the end of Winifred Meany's newspaper account.

Those eighth-grade schoolchildren would have marched out of St. Mary's Church, crossed Menasha Street and entered the cemetery, then fenced and gated to keep the farm animals out on Reedsville's Fair Days when cattle were running the streets. Her classmates then laid the young maiden to her final rest the Thursday after Christmas 1926.

If you walk across the road from St. Mary's Church, you will find a large white angel resting on a granite tombstone measuring just over six feet in height. A close-up of Cecilia's face is fixed on the grave as a lasting memorial to John and Anna's daughter—the third child to die in the Burich family.

As these events on that day unfolded, Anna cried profusely as she laid her third child in a grave.

While some people today are concerned about the side effects of vaccines, John and Anna likely would have given up their farm to have the polio vaccine, which was later developed by Jonas Salk in the 1950s. These vaccines eventually put the deadly virus at bay worldwide. The development of that vaccine was brought about when Franklin Delano Roosevelt helped to found the National Foundation for Infantile Paralysis. That foundation later became known as the March of Dimes.

Stricken by polio in 1921, Roosevelt had a passion for combatting the disease that eventually led the March of Dimes to become America's second-largest charity, with only the Red Cross topping it at the time. Millions of people literally donated dimes, collecting hundreds of millions of dollars for the organization.

As a young boy, I remember the March of Dimes donation cards circulating through Rockland Township, some of those fundraising efforts started in honor of Rockland's very own Cecilia Burich, a young soul lost far too early on her earthly journey.

# 20

# AND THEY DANCED

G et busy living or get busy dying!"
Morgan Freeman proclaims that line in the movie *Shawshank Redemption* after reflecting on a major crossroads decision in his life. It's one of my all-time favorite movie lines, as Freeman's character, Ellis "Red" Redding, gives advice to his wrongfully convicted prison friend Andy Dufresne, who is played by Tim Robbins.

I'd like to think those same thoughts—Get busy living or get busy dying—were going through Anna and John Burich's minds after burying a third child the Christmas season of 1926.

"Get busy living." That was John and Anna's choice.

The couple carried on with the construction of the family's second major livestock barn. This particular barn had an open haymow concept, allowing the Burich family to more easily store loose hay compared to their older barn built when John was a child. Remember, a baler to tightly compress hay wasn't available to the masses.

"That was a pretty big project building that barn," said John and Anna's daughter Julia.

"Pa's uncle Louis Turensky sawed all the lumber for the new barn. The homegrown trees came from the pine woods directly across the road," recalled Julia.

Based on photos, the barn went up in an orchestrated fashion after the masons completed the foundation. The wood frame sprouted like a new crop of spring dandelions thanks to neighbors who served as builders.

On this day, twenty-four men were either dangling from the rafters or passing beams up one side, while another crew was slapping and nailing boards on another side of the new Burich barn. *Author's collection.*

## The Peppy Three Played Until Dawn

"They had one big barn dance after it was completed," said Julia, who smiled as if it had happened just last night. "I was just about ten years old then…old enough to know how to dance," Julia said. Julia loved her waltzes and polkas.

"The band was The Peppy Three featuring three Sharbuck brothers. The Burich women and all their relatives made a full Bohemian-style meal, complete with kolaches. All the people ate their fill," said Julia.

Kolaches are as Bohemian as a food gets. Part of the word's meaning originates from the Czech language as *kolo*, meaning "circle" or "wheel." As for the rest, kolaches are a comfort food made of puffy dough, and their centers often contain fruit. Kolaches were originally a wedding dessert and would be served on special occasions. For the Burich family, a completed barn raising most definitely fit the special occasion checklist.

Given it was the heart of Prohibition, beer and liquor were hard to come by. But not that night! John had secured some beer and "brown bag specials" as John thanked the builder neighbors for getting the barn constructed in time for the first crop of hay.

The source of those spirits?

While Tom "had died," he was either supplying his brother from his Northeast Wisconsin–to–Chicago bootlegger route or John had another resource.

Back to that dance. It definitely was a peppy evening, as the party roared all night long until the roosters crowed the next dawn.

## DANCE HALLS PEPPERED THE AREA

If you were a teenager in the 1920s and 1930s, the local dance halls were the place to be. People literally filled a card with names of those they planned to dance with in pursuit of finding a future spouse. Married couples also danced the night away with family, friends and neighbors.

"Since the early 1900's when it began to take shape, until now [1976] when it has matured but not wilted, it has successfully quenched a thirst for music," wrote Robert Janda in a monograph series on bands in Manitowoc County.

"When combined with a dance step or an occasional nip of beer, its old-time rhythms have made arthritis disappear. Old-time music (also referred to as polka music) created plenty of excitement here and this is one big reason why Manitowoc has been called the pride of the polka belt," continued Janda.

That polka belt extended far into rural Manitowoc and Calumet Counties. The Bohemians, Polish, Belgians and Germans loved dancing and listening to their native countries' songs. These days, similar music is making a rebound with the influx of Mexican and other Latin American immigrants.

## "BANDS I LIKE"

"Don Schleis, Dick Rogers, Gene Hier, Lawrence Duchow, Dick Metko, Elroy Berkholtz, Joe Karman, and Romy Gosz," wrote Julia in her many journals. "Joe Karman's Mayflower Waltz and Flying Birds Waltz are among my favorites," she continued. "The Twilight Waltz is my favorite to dance with Randy," she added in her journal in reference to her son-in-law Randy Geiger, who married her daughter Rosalie.

"Our favorite dance spots as teenagers were Highway Ten, Kubale's, Reedsville's Legion Hall, and Buboltz's Grove. Another popular Bohemian hangout in the day was Homestead Tavern in Polifka Corners near the little village of Kellnersville." Dancing and social gatherings were clearly important to the Burich sisters.

"We learned to love music from our dad," wrote Julia about her father, John. "He loved to play an old-style concertina or accordion. It didn't have piano keys; it was the regular button style."

"He often played on the front porch on Sunday evening after the cows were milked. With very little traffic to cause road noise, the music would carry quite a fair distance," wrote Julia in her journal. "We [the girls] would dance while Pa played and after songs were done, we could hear neighbors clapping in the distance as Pa's nightly music routine was a neighborhood mainstay."

"We all had our weddings at home and then we held dances at nearby halls," Julia penned. "Sisters Agnes and Mary held their wedding dances at Kubale's Hall in Reedsville. Sister Beatie had hers at Kellnersville. Elmer and I had our dance at Reedsville's Legion Hall."

"Elmer and I were married June 16, 1938. We had our wedding at home on the farm with relatives and neighbors working on the meals," recalled Julia of her wedding day. "We had a breakfast for the bridal party, dinner at noon, and a supper, too. We had fifty guests for supper. The ceremony was held in the morning at St. Mary's and violins played as my dad walked me down the aisle less than a year before he died.

"A wedding dance was held from 9:00 p.m. to 1:00 a.m. All from our church were invited and the greater farming community. Romy Gosz furnished the music," stated Julia. Of course, those of Bohemian heritage simply loved hearing Romy and his orchestra as they pumped out rich Bohemian-style polka music.

Elmer and Julia's wedding would be one of the last at Reedsville's famed American Legion Hall. as it burned to the ground in January 1940 after a basketball game versus Brillion High School.

## Grimms Boy a Legend

To get Romy Gosz for a wedding dance in those days was a big coup. Between 1933 and 1938, the Gosz boys cut seventy-four records. Romy, who was born in Grimms, Wisconsin, in 1910, played fifty consecutive nights throughout the area at the time.

Internationally known as the "Polka King," Gosz had records recorded by Universal, Mercury, Broadway and a host of other labels. He even appeared in *Time* and *Life* magazines.

The "RG" on those bandstands represent the famed Romy Gosz Band. Gosz and his band would have folks dancing as if it were New Year's Eve every night. *Author's collection.*

Some Gosz band engagements brought upward of 1,600 people to dance halls and parks. He was a child prodigy, having landed his first dance job at age seven after just one piano lesson. This was the only lesson he would ever take.

"People would be going at midnight like it was New Year's Eve," said Dan Zahorik, a member of Romy's band, in a 1976 interview with Robert Janda.

And so, they danced.

# 21

# REO Speed Wagon to the Rescue

"Weee-oooo."
"Weee-oooo."

The iconic, long-lasting wail that emanates from fire trucks has been seared into nearly everyone's psyche. It brings a range of emotions that dance through one's mind just like the flames those fire trucks douse with water. For those whose property is ablaze, the sound offers hope the fire will soon be out. To those in an accident, the wail of a fire truck offers promise of rescue. For young boys and girls watching a parade, it's a joyful sound that signals the start of a grand celebration.

However, have you ever pondered why fire trucks start out parades?

Certainly, fire trucks are the source of civic pride. It's a way to honor the men and women who put themselves in harm's way to rescue others. When fire trucks from nearby departments join the procession, it represents solidarity as neighboring volunteer fire departments routinely offer aid in emergencies.

But there's likely another reason.

In the pioneer days, there were little to no tax dollars available to fund fire protection. Not only did these brave souls pull their own fire equipment to the scene in the early 1900s, but firemen also went door to door asking for donations to fund equipment purchases.

So, going back to the pioneer times, firemen led those parades so donors could see the new purchases on display—shiny, new and ready to protect.

## John Bought Fire Protection

John and Anna Burich kept a metal money box that held the family farm's most important documents, including every land transfer and will for the Burich family dating back to 1867. In that same security box, a fire protection certificate was reverently placed. That certificate remains in pristine condition, and it speaks volumes to what some rural farmers thought about fighting fire. It reads:

> *This is to certify that John A. Burich whose property is located at West one half of the Northwest quarter, Section 4, Township 19, Range 21 East, has donated $35.00 towards the Boyer Fire Apparatus purchased for Reedsville and Community, with the assurance made by the village board that his fire-call shall be answered with from three to six firemen as quickly as it is possible to get there with the fire truck.*
>
> *In case of fire in the village and the country at the same time, the fire truck, with enough men to operate it, will answer the country call. There are to be no further charges to subscribers except to pay each fireman $1.00 per hour on a call.*
>
> *This agreement shall be in force during the life of the above mentioned fire truck only. This certificate is not transferable to another location.*
> *Signed, Harry A. Krueger, Clerk*
> *Signed, Arnold F. Rusch, President*

Despite the incredible detail in that fire protection certificate, it bears no date. That sent me digging for details. While Reedsville was incorporated in 1892, its fire department did not take root until 1895, when C.G. Hagenow was appointed the first fire chief. The very next year, Herman Boettcher took over the reins.

In the early days, the firemen were summoned to an emergency by a fire bell located at the old village hall located on Manitowoc Street. Those firemen pulled firefighting equipment by hand or borrowed horses for longer runs. It was tough work.

In 1927, the department acquired its first motor-driven truck, an REO Speed Wagon fire truck. Chief Herman Boettcher and the eleven other firemen were more effective with that unit. Not only were they able to reach the fire scene much faster, but their energy would also be used for firefighting, instead of pulling water pumps.

## FIRE PROTECTION CERTIFICATE

**THIS IS TO CERTIFY that** *John J. Burich*
**WHOSE PROPERTY IS LOCATED** *West one half of Northwest quarter, Sec. 4, Township 19, Range 21 East*
**HAS DONATED $35.00 TOWARDS THE BOYER FIRE APPARATUS PURCHASED FOR REEDSVILLE AND COMMUNITY, WITH THE ASSURANCE MADE BY THE VILLAGE BOARD THAT HIS FIRE-CALL SHALL BE ANSWERED WITH FROM THREE TO SIX FIREMEN AS QUICKLY AS IT IS POSSIBLE TO GET THERE WITH THE FIRE TRUCK.**

In case of fire in the village and the country at the same time, the fire truck, with enough men to operate it, will answer the country call. There are to be no further charges to subscribers except to pay each fireman $1.00 per hour on a call.

This agreement shall be in force during the life of the above mentioned fire truck only. This certificate is not transferable to another location.

VILLAGE OF REEDSVILLE.

_____ Clerk    _____ President.

This 1927 certificate signed by officials for the Village of Reedsville recognized John Burich's thirty-five-dollar donation for the new REO Speed Wagon equipped with a Boyer Fire Apparatus. *Author's collection.*

## WHAT WAS IT CALLED?

While village and fire department history chronicles the purchase of an "REO Speed Wagon fire truck," the certificate signed by Krueger and Rusch held by our family calls it the "Boyer Fire Apparatus."

Which one is correct?

Long before the 1970s rock band **REO Speedwagon** bore the name, that 1927 REO Speed Wagon was built by the REO Motor Car Company, which ranked fifth in those days among U.S. automobile and truck manufacturers. REO were the initials of the company's founder, Ransom Eli Olds. He also invented the Oldsmobile automobile.

The 1927 model featured the unusual "T-6," six-cylinder engine. It used a six-volt chain-drive starter, mounted on the front of the transmission. The clutch had to be engaged and in neutral to crank the engine.

Once purchased by the Reedsville Fire Department, the REO Speed Wagon went from the Michigan manufacturing plant to Boyer Fire Apparatus Company in Logansport, Indiana, to be equipped for firefighting equipment and ornately decorated. Boyer built fire trucks on many different companies' chassis.

There you have it; both historic accounts are accurate, according to the magazine *Vintage Fire Truck & Equipment*.


# The Instigator

Arnold F. Rusch was quite a man based on all historic accounts. Born on May 4, 1888, near Brillion, he later became a prominent businessman in the village of Reedsville. He started a career as a lumberman in 1905 with his father. In 1912, they incorporated as A.H. Rusch and Sons Co. Arnold Rusch was a great civic-minded person.

In 1905, he organized Reedsville's first basketball team. He was a charter member of the Reedsville Chamber of Commerce and later held the office of secretary. He served as village trustee for two years and village president for seven years.

It's during that term as president that Rusch helped secure the new fire truck. The Village of Reedsville could not foot the bill alone. That's when Rusch turned toward those living in the surrounding countryside.


# A Big Donation

Rusch went from farm to farm asking for donations to buy a truck. John and Anna talked and then decided to give $35. John and Anna Burich paid $312.76 in taxes for their 197-acre farm back in 1930. Of those taxes, the largest chunk went to a new category—highway tax—$96.42. As for the remainder, $71.01 went to the township (Rockland), $66.10 went to schools, $64.86 went to the county (Manitowoc) and $14.37 went to the state (Wisconsin). That was based on a property valuation of $17,530.

By 1935, during the heart of the Great Depression, taxes plummeted 61 percent to just $121.11 on the same farm. So a $35 donation for Reedsville's new fire truck was a big deal.

As Reedsville was raising funds for its new fire truck, so was Brillion. City of Brillion residents would pay half the costs of a new motorized truck, with the rural townsfolk paying the other half. Fire protection in Brillion also cost thirty-five dollars—the same donation paid by John Burich.

President Rusch and his Reedsville village board, along with Chief Boettcher, went door-to-door in the surrounding Maple Grove and Rockland townships.

John and Anna were civic-minded, and by all accounts they gave readily to others. However, if you didn't have that certificate, the fire department would not respond if you had a fire. The donation was akin to buying fire insurance.

## THE BURICH FARM IS ON FIRE

Just a few years later, the Reedsville fire bell rang loudly, calling all to attention. To Reedsville's western horizon, black smoke billowed high into the sky.

"Whose farm is it?" asked one of the firemen.

"It's John Burich, and he has a fire certificate," one hollered out. With that, all twelve firemen loaded up on the REO Speed Wagon, with others in a motorcar, and sped down the gravel road.

Upon arriving on the scene, the firemen didn't know what to do. As it turns out, the John A. Burich farm was just fine. But directly across the road, the barn on the Joseph Burich family property was ablaze.

That farmer had passed on the thirty-five-dollar certificate and donation for Reedsville's new fire truck. By the rules of the day, the firemen were not to fight that fire.

By this time, a conclave of neighbors and firemen hastily met on the gravel road running north–south between the farms. "I know he didn't buy the certificate, but I did," said John A. Burich to fire chief Herman Boettcher. John had been anticipating the situation, knowing the terms of the area's fire protection.

"You do not have to haul water for this fire." Pleading the case on behalf of his neighbor, John got no response. "Cerpani vody z rybnika!" Red John Burich then exclaimed as the next plea rang out in John's Bohemian tongue for the assembled to hear.

Even those who didn't speak Bohemian already knew John A. Burich was telling the firemen to take water from his own farm's pond, leaving him without extra water during the parched Dirty Thirties. Of course, this was the height of the Great Depression, and water was a precious commodity.

Chief Boettcher broke with protocol and gave the order. At once, his fire brigade began setting up hoses from John's pond, ran them across the road and began extinguishing the flames. The firemen saved most of the property.

## TAXES TO THE RESCUE

That fire presented a mighty big quandary. The firefighters should not have responded to this fire because the farmer didn't pay thirty-five dollars for a fire protection certificate. Putting out that fire may have signaled to others that future donations were not necessary because the fire department would still answer the call.

By 1947, firefighters were no longer placed in that tough position.

That's because the nearby Collins Fire Department asked Rockland residents to pay $600 for fire protection for the southern portion of the township. Reedsville did the same for the northern part of the town of Rockland. Brillion followed suit in the western section of Rockland.

The next time area residents heard the unmistakable "Weee-oooo" sound ringing from a fire truck, there was no debate about fighting the fire. It was all hands on deck.

# 22

# BUILD YOUR OWN ROAD

When the first settlers arrived in Wisconsin, they would have been lucky to find a narrow trail created by the Native Americans through the wilderness. If such a trail did exist, travelers would only be able to ride a horse on it single file. As more settlers arrived, they began cutting one-lane wagon trails through the forest to reach new settlements.

Those primitive roads extended south from the Bay of Green Bay, west from Lake Michigan and east from Lake Winnebago, as waterways were the area's first highways. However, these dirt trails were a far cry from the roads we have grown accustomed to traveling. In spring, travelers often abandoned horse-drawn wagons that got stuck in the mud. In some cases, the traveler was forced to come back later with additional help to free the wagon.

## GRAVEL PITS POPPED UP EVERYWHERE

In Calumet and Manitowoc County's early settlement days, pioneers would use gravel to fill in potholes on primitive dirt roads. In other instances, early settlers filled in holes or gullies with wood logs or planks and put dirt back over the top to smooth the surface. For the most part, the road repairs were just enough to make the road somewhat passable when horses were the chief source of transportation.

Early roads were often one-lane trails. As transportation evolved from horse-drawn carts and wagons to automobiles, roads were widened and a gravel base was added to the roadbeds. *Author's collection.*

At the dawn of the automobile age, the responsibility of road improvement still fell into the hands of local residents. If you wanted an improved road, you built it yourself or partnered with neighbors by grading the surface and adding gravel. Ambitious neighborhoods even dug ditches to drain water away.

There were no municipalities with road crews handling this work.

Eventually, gravel evolved from an occasional need for filling a pothole to an absolute necessity for road construction as automobiles became the preferred mode of transportation. Local farmers throughout the area opened small gravel pits to meet demand. John Burich got in the gravel business, eventually opening three pits on his property. These pits were far from modern quarries filled with heavy earth-moving equipment.

There was also a second growing need for gravel and sand as Portland cement was entering its heyday. Sand and gravel were critical components for this new building material to pave roads, and farmers were purchasing cement to construct silos and cow yards and building foundations, as cement was far superior to lime mortar.

The same road maintenance program applied to snow removal. Drivers who wanted a passable road needed to get out there and plow it themselves.

As a child, John's daughter Julia recalled her father hitching the horses on a Sunday morning. That was after hand-milking twenty-four cows. He would plow the two-mile stretch of township road to Reedsville, where local villagers had opened the remainder of the road.

John then returned home, widening the road a bit more with his second pass. By then, his wife, Anna, and five daughters all climbed into the family's Black Buick and drove to church.

Those who lived beyond the Burich farm would plow up to his property line, and the neighborhood plowing effort eventually extended throughout the Rockland Township.

## BETTER ROADS EQUAL BETTER BUSINESS

The first recorded request to improve Reedsville roads came in the early 1890s. Mr. Kabat, a Reedsville saloonkeeper, requested that the town clear dirt and mud away from his saloon so that men could tie up their horses and stop in for a cool beverage on a hot day. Manitowoc Street later became Reedsville's first paved road in 1928, according to *History of Reedsville to 1976*.

One year earlier, Brillion began paving its Main Street, according to *Brillion 1885 to 2010*. Brillion received some money from Calumet County since its main drag also doubled as State Highway 114. Like farmers placing gravel on roads at their own cost, local business owners footed part of the paving bill for the 1927 Brillion main street project, as county and city funds did not cover the full costs.

## WISCONSIN WAS A ROAD LEADER

Roads did not have names in the early 1900s. Wisconsin pioneered naming mechanisms, becoming the first state in the nation and the first region of the world to have a numbered highway system. Michigan quickly followed.

In 1917, the Wisconsin legislature established the State Highway Commission, and it laid out five thousand miles of numbered highways on paper. The very next year—in just one week during May 1918—signage went up on those routes. By 1923, the coverage of Wisconsin's state highways had doubled to ten thousand miles.

In 1926, the federal government started the U.S. Highway System and reassigned a number of Wisconsin roadways. That included renaming U.S. Highway 10. Prior to its new name, the road was called State Trunk Highway 12 for one short decade. After U.S. 10 received its new name, the grandest paving project the area had ever seen started to take place.

In May 1933, U.S. Highway 10 was paved from Reedsville to State Highway 55 near Menasha. By September, it had been completed, and 2,500 people attended the ribbon-cutting ceremony on Highway 10 on the Manitowoc-Calumet County line, reported *The Brillion News*. That new highway was a generational changing event.

Just how important were these paved roadways? When the roads improved, it was a quick transition for passengers away from the railroad, reported in the *History of Collins*. By the 1930s, trucks and cars had taken over, and passenger train service began to dry up. Also, with more cars came more paved roads.

## DAIRY DEMANDED GOOD ROADS

The area was simply following the trends of major metropolitan areas. By 1920, Milwaukee County had 154 miles of concrete road, according to the March 1920 *Concrete Highway Magazine*, published by the Portland Cement Association. At that time, a snow removal fund was created in Wisconsin's most densely populated county. Three four-wheel-drive army trucks moved snow.

"As a result of this work, Milwaukee County highways are open all year round for travel," wrote William Cavanaugh, Milwaukee's highway commissioner. "Milk and other farm produce are hauled to town over them through the winter, an important item when it is known that more than 65 percent of milk and dairy products entering Milwaukee throughout the year are hauled by motor truck."

Yes, both the automobile and Wisconsin's growing dairy industry helped drive the need for paved roads. After all, in 1914, Wisconsin had overtaken New York to become the nation's largest dairy state. And a growing number of those dairy products had to be shipped well beyond the Badger State's borders.

Wisconsin's network of roads was helping cement its growing national reputation as the land of Cheeseheads.

# 23

# ALL YOUR HORSE CAN PULL
# FOR SEVENTY CENTS

People preferred the convenience and freedom of cars. Milk and cheese and other farm-raised produce arrived in the cities more quickly by truck than train.

John Burich was more than happy to fuel the road building business by selling sand and gravel from his land. To keep up with booming sales, John opened a third gravel pit on his farm. February happened to be John's biggest sales month.

Why February? By Únor—that's Bohemian for February—winter was starting to loosen its grip on the landscape with its growing day length. Únor translates to "melting ice," and the spring thaw would soon create roadbed potholes. At the same time, there was still enough snow and ice to run a sleigh. That allowed customers to easily skid heavy horse-drawn sleighs loaded with heavy gravel to their final destination.

Moving gravel was extremely labor-intensive in Wisconsin's pioneer days. Like everything else, sleds had to be filled by hand—one shovel scoop at a time. John would loosen the frozen gravel for his customers with the blasting power of dynamite. On a few occasions, his daughter Julia would recall her father coming into the house with blood oozing from open wounds on his face and hands.

"Po nastavení pojistky se nedostala dost daleko," he told his wife, Anna, in the native Bohemian tongue that the family still spoke. Daughter Julia, a grade school student who also spoke both Bohemian and English, knew he said, "Didn't get far enough away after setting the fuse!"

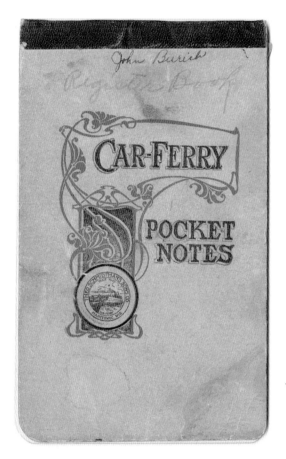

John Burich recorded all his gravel sales in this notebook produced by the Theodore Schmidtman Company of nearby Manitowoc, Wisconsin. *Author's collection.*

John Burich recorded all his gravel sales in a notebook produced by the Theodore Schmidtman Company of nearby Manitowoc that imprinted its "Car Ferry" logo on its branded items. John's particular ledger was printed after 1925, when the Schmidtman Company purchased its own press to print ledgers. A few years later, the Schmidtman Company added a ruling machine to print colored line paper. The company closed its doors in 1990.

Based on sales recorded in John's ledger book, which survives to this day, he was doing a whole lot of blasting in those pits in 1929. Anna and her four daughters could feel the house rattle and see the windows vibrate due to shockwaves from the explosions. John set off dynamite to free frozen gravel as he sold load after load.

## NEARLY 350 LOADS IN SIX WEEKS

John charged seventy cents per two-horse-drawn-sled load. If you had strong horses, you got a deal based on those prices. If your horses were weaker than the average team, that wasn't John's concern—he charged the same rate. John did have some compassion if a farmer came with a small cart and often adjusted the rate to twenty-five to fifty cents per load depending on the size of the vehicle.

John, who had only a second-grade education, kept the math simple in his ledger. Anna would handle it from there, often sending the bills and correcting the spelling of each person's name—often a muddled mess of Bohemian and English.

Who were the customers?

| | |
|---|---|
| William Behnke | total bill $2.00, four small loads in a wood cart (hence the reduced fifty-cent fee per load) |
| Reinhart Bessert | $3.50, five trips |
| Frederick Bubolz | $12.60, eighteen loads |
| Albert Fischer, Evergreen Hill Dairy Farm | $18.20, twenty-six loads hauled from February 21 to March 2 |
| Stephen Foreyt | $2.80, four sleighs |
| Adolph Haelfrish | $4.90, seven sleighs |
| Joseph Jerabek | $2.80, four loads |
| John Kocourek | $1.40, two loads |
| Hubert Krainik | $7.00, ten loads |
| Robert Krepline | $19.60, twenty-eight loads, making Krepline John's third-best customer that year |
| Willie Krueger | $11.20, sixteen loads |
| Albert Prochnow | $1.40, two sleighs |
| Edwin Reinke, Twilight Farm | $1.25, five small loads in a wood cart |

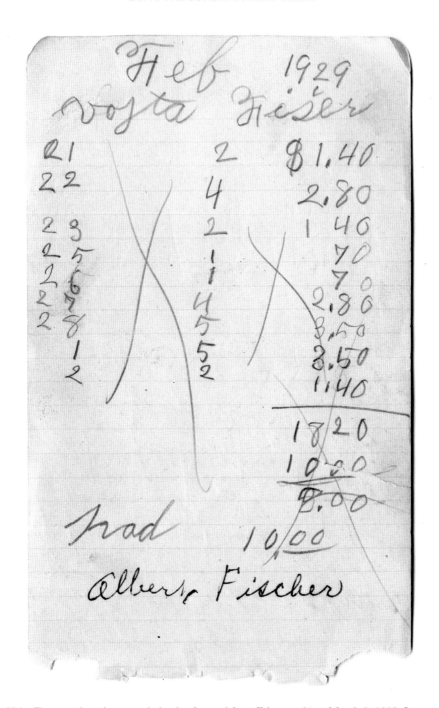

Vojta Fiser purchased twenty-six loads of gravel from February 21 to March 2, 1929. Later, John Burich's wife, Anna, would record the buyer's name in English by writing "Albert Fischer." *Author's collection.*

| | |
|---|---|
| Otto Reinke | $37.10, fifty-three loads, making Otto John's second-best customer |
| Richard Reinke | $6.30, nine loads |
| Arno Schmidt | $4.20, six loads |
| John Schmidt | $7.00, ten loads |
| Henry Schultz | $16.10, twenty-three loads |
| Art Sonnabend | $2.10, three loads |
| William Rusch | $70.00, one hundred loads, making him the best customer in 1929 |
| Joseph Vondrachek | $5.50, eleven small loads in a wood cart |

These sales represented an incredible flurry of 346 loads during a six-week window starting in early February 1929.

## SALES CRASHED IN 1930

Just one year later, sales dropped off sharply as the Great Depression gripped the area. John Burich recorded a meager $27.50 in gravel sales to Arno Schmidt, Hubert Labitzke and William Labityke. The latter two men farmed just south of Long Lake.

When good times were rolling in 1929, the Burich gravel pit netted $237.25 in sales. The 1930 sales crash represented an 88 percent downturn from the prior year. Just like that, John's gravel sales dried up like the Great Depression's missing rains.

# 24

# BOOM GOES THE DYNAMITE

Horses, a pickaxe, a shovel, fire and, of course, brute human strength. This is the short list of the tools and power sources that immigrant farmers had at their disposal to clear the stump-infested, rock-littered land before growing their first crops. It was backbreaking work.

That began to evolve in 1866, one year before the Burich family settled in the Reedsville area. A product far more destructive than gunpowder had been developed. While the invention did its job, there were major, even deadly, issues associated with its use.

In the 1860s, the Italian chemist Ascanio Sobrero invented nitroglycerine, which had incredible blasting capabilities. However, it lacked stability. When nitroglycerine began to break down, an explosion soon followed.

As the Transcontinental Railroad linking Omaha, Nebraska, and San Francisco, California, began emanating from its two points of origin in 1866 after the Civil War, builders began shipping nitroglycerine to San Francisco to expedite construction and link the growing democracy. To get nitroglycerine from East Coast manufacturing plants to the Pacific Ocean port town of San Francisco, it was packed in shipping crates leaving New York City via a steamship. It was offloaded and carted across the Isthmus of Panama. In that era, that isthmus was still a land route. That nitroglycerine was reloaded on another oceangoing steamer and shipped to its final destination.

On one such occasion, a two-and-a-half-foot-square crate was leaking an oily substance upon arriving in San Francisco. Who was to blame? To determine what had happened, officials from the steamship company and the consigner, Wells Fargo, met at the Wells Fargo office on Montgomery Street. To settle the question about who was at fault for the leak, a Wells Fargo employee grabbed a chisel and a hammer and began to open the leaking crate.

BOOM!

All the workers were killed instantly, and the Wells Fargo building on Montgomery Street was leveled to the ground. Buildings over a quarter mile away rattled on Monday, April 16, 1866.

That didn't stop railroad builders who ordered more nitroglycerine. They blasted through the Sierra Nevada Mountain range and its granite rock. With more shipments, more unplanned, premature explosions ensued.

The death toll mounted. The situation got so deadly that the California legislature banned the transport of liquid nitroglycerine into the Bear Flag Republic.

## Along Comes "Safety Powder"

Even with all the deaths, nitroglycerine got the work done far more quickly than a pickaxe, shovel and gunpowder. And with no such thing as modern-day bulldozers, a Swedish chemist named Alfred Nobel continued his pursuit to create a shelf-stable nitroglycerine product. He did so even after nitroglycerine killed his brother Emil in a devastating explosion.

Nobel eventually created a nitroglycerine product with sorbents such as powdered shells, clay and other stabilizers. Along this journey, he invented a detonator and a blasting cap. Before applying for patents, he needed a name.

Nobel demonstrated his invention for the first time at a quarry in Redhill Surrey, England. Due to the many mishaps on the journey to the product's introduction, Nobel initially wanted to name his product "Nobel's Safety Powder." However, after the successful demonstration in England, he settled on "dynamite," referring to the Greek word for "power," as demonstrating his invention's explosive capabilities mattered more than safety.

Dynamite's popularity exploded, sweeping across Europe and North America. Dynamite became the product of choice to clear land, mine minerals and blast away rock to build roadbeds and tunnels. Nobel's fame grew, and eventually his estate established what became known as the Nobel Peace Prize.

## Farming with Dynamite

While I have not unearthed a copy of the book *Farming with Dynamite: A Few Hints to Farmers*, published by the DuPont Corporation of Wilmington, Delaware, in the family archives, John Burich likely had a copy of it. The 1910 book suggested the following:

> *Dynamite is very powerful, much more so than gunpowder, but is actually safer to handle. The purpose of this booklet is to tell you the wonderful value of the use of "Red Cross Dynamite" on the farm.*
>
> *The chief uses are mentioned below and are explained in detail further on. Complete instructions are furnished in the Handbook of Explosives for Farmers, Planters and Ranchers.*

> - *Clearing of stumps, trees, and boulders*
> - *Breaking up hard-pan, shale, or clay subsoils*
> - *Plowing*
> - *Planting and cultivating orchards*
> - *Digging ditches, post holes, wells, and reservoirs*

King and Billy pulled stumps, plowed ground and hauled supplies—including dynamite—to the gravel pit. Longtime Burich Farm "hired man" Frank Shimek is driving the team. *Author's collection.*

- *Road-making and grading*
- *Excavating cellars and foundation trenches*
- *Regenerating old, worn-out farms*

"You can dynamite all those stumps for about one-third the cost of pulling and chopping them," wrote the DuPont corporation, further making its case. That statement alone might not have hooked a frugal farmer like John Burich when he took over the farm in the early 1900s. But the next two points surely caught his attention: "You can blast fifty stumps in the time it would take you to pull and chop up one or two. One man could do all the work, if necessary."

John Burich had a wife and only daughters. That last line in the DuPont book definitely appealed to him. No way he was risking the Burich women's lives blowing up stumps when he could do it all by himself.

And John blasted. It started with stumps and moved on to gravel. At times, John's blasting became a daily endeavor.

## Dynamite Brought Water

During the Dirty Thirties, John searched out greener pastures and a water source for his heifers. That caused him and his sons-in-law from the Kalies and Sleger families to gather heifers for a cattle drive. So desperate were his new sons-in-law for forage and water that they herded cattle from Askeaton and Kellnersville, both traveling nearly fourteen miles to get to the Burich farm. This travel was done on foot.

"Herding the cattle was the difficult part," said John's daughter Julia.

"Watering heifers was pretty easy," she chuckled.

"Pa found a spring down there," she said of his forty-acre parcel in the modern-day Collins Marsh, which is now a wildlife sanctuary. "Out came his dynamite. Pa set off a charge."

BOOM!

Dirt and debris flew high into the air. Those heifers later had a pond and all the water that they could ever drink.

# 25

# EVERYTHING BUT THE SQUEAL

While meatpacking mogul Gustavus Swift may have coined the phrase, "Now we use all of the hog except his grunt [squeal]," European immigrants arriving in America had already put that into practice every time they processed an animal on their farms or had the task carried out at the local butcher shops that dotted rural communities. That included meat markets steeped with Bohemian, German, Irish and other European traditions located throughout the United States.

So, what's the meaning of "using everything but the grunt or squeal"?

Simply said, food was a precious resource.

When Mom or Grandma said, "Clean your plate," they meant it. Those women and others like them did not want to waste food, and sometimes adults didn't know where the next meal would come from to feed the family.

Hardworking farmers also wanted to instill in the youth exactly how much work, energy and resources went into growing and harvesting that food. With all that in mind, every part of the animal—except the sounds they made—had a purpose in the immigrant home.

For Gustavus Swift, the phrase "using everything but the squeal" was a business directive as he built his meatpacking empire. He wanted to wring the last penny of value out of the animal's carcass.

## OLD-WORLD PICKLED FAVORITES

If you go to a rural Wisconsin tavern, you might still get a glimpse of foods that our immigrant relatives ate. These foods are a mere novelty these days. In the late 1800s and early 1900s, these foods provided much-needed calories and in some cases were even considered delicacies.

- Pickled gizzards from chickens, turkeys, geese and ducks
- Pickled eggs from every poultry species imaginable
- Pickled hog hocks and hog feet
- Pickled herring
- Sausage and bologna

The list goes on.

Those would be among the novelties found in local meat shops or Wisconsin taverns that carry on Old World traditions. However, many among us would thumb our noses at eating such foods on a daily basis, as our palates have evolved beyond these lesser cuts of meats. For old-timers, however, those were the foods of their youth.

Cured meats and sausage were the backbone of butcher shop sales. The curing and pickling process extended the shelf life of meat without refrigeration. *Author's collection.*

When cleaning out my grandparents' Elmer and Julia Pritzl's home, they still had saws, knives and sausage-making equipment. My late uncle Elmer John "Butch" Pritzl quickly claimed the sausage maker, knowing the great traditions it represented and the actual sausage making he witnessed as a child. These included making liverwurst or leburwurst and blood sausage.

This made a great deal of sense in many ways. For starters, Butch loved eating liverwurst. Secondly, Uncle Butch bore the names of his mother Julia's two most loved men: Elmer, her husband, and John Burich, her father. As a result, Butch learned a great many Old World food-making traditions.

## China Travels Provide Context

For Americans of this century, it's hard to fathom eating some of these foods. To be fair, some of these entrées even cause me to cringe. Three trips to China from 2017 to 2019 changed my thinking, however, as I tried a wide variety of dishes. Reflecting on these meals, I think John and Anna Burich and their children may have said "Bon appétit."

Nearly all the foods I ate in China were splendid. Now, I likely had cuisine offered to the higher end of Chinese society, as my travels were geared toward launching a Chinese edition of the *Hoard's Dairyman* magazine. Even so, I witnessed a great deal traveling far beyond China's modern coast to the Shaanxi province, where plumbing had yet to reach homes occupied by many of its citizens. That meant human excrement was flowing in ditches just as it did in cities centuries ago. And a few blocks away were modern high-rise buildings sprouting like dandelions in spring.

It was a stark contrast.

In nearly all the regions I traveled, some form of an animal blood entrée could be ordered at any meal. Some animal blood dishes had a liquid element, while others are served up in a solid form like Jell-O. To my eye, it looked to be duck, lamb or pig blood—it tasted a bit minerally or grainy in texture.

Fried chicken's feet were a favorite dish for many Chinese. Not much imagination here. Cut off the chicken's feet and deep fry them. Not many calories and a lot of crunching. After my first chicken foot, I was satisfied not to try another.

Another food that fit in the same category was deep-fried tendons—that's the portion of the animal that connects muscle to bone. A tough and fibrous food, it's rather cheap and was like chewing a small tree twig.

On one occasion, I ate a donkey burger. Quite frankly, I would eat another, as it tasted like beef from a cow to me. Then there was my Sunday night dinner of duck tongue. I was able to navigate my chopsticks to eat about five before moving on.

These stories help place the diets of immigrant America into context. Money was scarce, as was food. You ate what was on your plate.

As a teenage boy who had just obtained a driver's license, I remember returning from sucker fishing one evening. Having cleaned my fresh catch, I brought it to my then eighty-year-old grandparents, Elmer and Julia.

"Where are the eggs?" asked Grandma looking at the cleaned fillets. Naturally, the fish had been cleaned and the guts were gone.

"Who would bring an uncleaned fish as a gift?" I thought to myself. But Grandma wasn't joking when she asked the question. "You wasted the best part, Corey! I would have fried those eggs or ate them raw!" she said of the suckers caught during the spring spawning run.

Grandpa Elmer thanked me for the fish and then said, "Next time just bring them here, and we will clean them ourselves." Talk about using the whole fish! Well, at least most of it.

So, our ancestors ate everything but the squeal just like people in China do to this very day.

While most of Europe uses the modern-day calendar with months labeled January, February, March and so forth, that was not the case in old Bohemia. A stroll through immigrant cemeteries of Bohemian descent will shed further meaning on the words chosen by that nationality.

Life centered on food and its harvest.

- Prosinec, the month of December, descends from the Slavic word *prasata*, the month to slaughter pigs.
- October, rijen, is rutting season for deer.
- August, srpen, is the month to harvest.
- July, cervenec, is the month of ripening.
- May, kveten, is the month of flowering.

## LOCAL MEAT MARKETS

Until the passage of the Meat Inspection Act of 1906, meat processing was an unregulated industry like America's largely lawless Wild West of those days. While people can process animals for their own use at home in modern times, all salable meat must be processed by state or federally inspected facilities.

Even with the passage of the Meat Inspection Act of 1906 and its subsequent regulation, butcher shops still stood everywhere. In 1923, the Milwaukee city directory listed over seven hundred such shops, according to Milwaukee historian John Gurda. It's these German, Bohemian and Polish immigrants who formed the link-loving regions and grew Wisconsin's culture of sausage. Each ethnic group brought with them Old World recipes.

Sausage and pickling were important ways to preserve meat in the days before refrigeration and freezers.

While every small community had its own butcher shop, Brillion is among the only in the area that still survives to this day. The Kanter family ran the Palace Meat Market until Otto Arndt took full ownership in 1945. Otto's son Clayton later joined the operation and moved the business from Brillion's Main Street to U.S. Highway 10. During that time, the Palace Meat Market was rebranded Arndt's Meat Market. In 1998, Chuck and Linda Roehrborn took over the business, retaining many of Arndt's famous recipes and adding award winners of their own.

Brillion had other meat markets, including Hesser's Meat Market, which set up its storefront in 1898. That business continued to carry meat until the mid-1970s, when Great-Uncle Elmer Geiger was the last to own it.

Ducks and geese were mainstays on the Burich and Pritzl farm. While some waterfowl eventually made it onto the family table, others were sold to Reedsville's Kadow Market. *Author's collection.*

Various versions of Reedsville's Kadow Market operated on Manitowoc Street from 1926 to 1965. Besides carrying a retail meat business, the Reedsville market brought rural veal and poultry to the city markets. The Burich and Pritzl families, who raised ducks and geese, provided waterfowl to this Reedsville business. Later the business was known as the Kuether-Kadow Market.

Collins boasted the Schneider Butcher Shop owned by Charles Schneider. It ran from the early 1900s to the 1940s until both the butcher shop and smokehouse were demolished. The nearby towns of Whitelaw, Valders and Potter also had butcher shops.

While some of these butcher shops are a distant memory, Wisconsin still has the rich tradition of preparing meats. The University of Wisconsin–Madison boasts the nation's only Master Meat Crafter Program. It is highly regarded and a first-of-its-kind meat industry training program offered by the University of Wisconsin–Madison Meat Science Department designed to provide participants with in-depth and comprehensive knowledge of meat science, food safety and processing. At the completion of the two-year program, graduates earn the distinction of a "Master Meat Crafter."

## What's a Locker Plant?

The Schuh Apartments, which date back to 1849, are detailed in the *History of the Town of Maple Grove*. By 1870, a small store was set up in the hamlet of Maple Grove by J.P. Sheahan. Four years later, the Maple Grove post office set up shop there, too. A saloon was quickly added to capture revenue from the daily foot traffic as people came to get their mail, and then an ice cream parlor joined the expansive business by 1910.

Everything ground to a halt during Prohibition. After booze was legal again in 1933, John Dvorak purchased the store and saloon. Dvorak also put in a locker plant.

"Locker plant?" I asked my father, Randy Geiger.

"Oh yes, before people could buy freezers for their homes, you rented part of a cold locker room to store butchered meat and pork. Our family had a space there when I was a child."

There were about four hundred rented boxes to store your butchered meat. In 1948, Art and Clara Dietrich purchased the business and operated it until 1962. Robert and Margaret Schuh bought the store, tavern, locker plant and residence in 1962. As people started buying their own freezers, the locker plant was discontinued in 1969. The store closed in 1974.

Kabat's Country Gardens in Reedsville also had meat lockers. On June 25, 1937, Kabat's installed 408 food lockers that became an asset to the community. In those days, brother Ignatius "Ig" was the tavern keeper, brother William the harness maker and brother Joseph the shoe repairman. The William Kabat family resided in the living quarters above the tavern. Elmer and Julia were patrons of the Kabat facility, storing meat there.

Butchering was a neighborhood activity that often started after morning milking with the hopes of wrapping up meat processing before the night's chores began. The Burich family homestead basement had an ample work area, access to water and a modern sewer system, which made it perfect for processing meat.

"June 24, 1947, we butchered one pig with Adolph Burich. It took a half a day and that one pig provided enough meat for the entire summer," wrote Grandma Julia in her journal.

Knowing the frugality of my grandparents and their dairy-farm neighbors who helped that day, they certainly used everything but the squeal.

# 26

# A Carp for Christmas

Pojďme mít kapra na Vánoce!"

To this very day, you will still hear people throughout Czechoslovakia declare, "Let's have carp for Christmas!"

That's right, the rough fish that Americans thumb their nose at these days is considered food for royalty and craved by families alike—not only in the Czech Republic but also throughout much of Europe.

On the days leading up to Christmas, in many parts of Europe, carp are sold at markets in town centers. At these markets, shoppers will size the carp up as they swim in huge barrels placed along the street by vendors.

While a growing number of shoppers have the merchants kill and clean their prize fish selection, a number of the natives still prefer the traditional route of bringing the fish home and placing it in the bathtub to swim about until Christmas Day dinner. This process ensures the freshest fish possible for the family and dates back centuries.

For Europeans, a carp dinner would be craved as much as Americans enjoy ham, turkey or even steak.

## Royal Carp

In Asia, carp has been raised as an important food source and garden element for nearly four thousand years. The carp has been a revered food

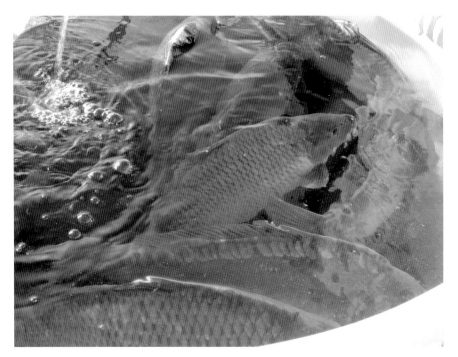

Unlike the carp in America, carp in Europe spend their final months in clear water, free of algae. It's this system that greatly adds to their flavor. *istock.*

source in Europe for well over one thousand years. While Europe's carp and those found throughout North America originate from the same genetic lines, that's where the commonalities cease.

Records indicate that carp began being farmed by Austrian nobility in the 1200s. It's believed that those carp originated from Asia via trade routes through the Middle East. From Austria, carp spread throughout Europe in the Middle Ages and reached England by 1496. When some farm-raised carp escaped ponds, King Henry VIII offered rewards to those in the countryside who could bring "carps to the king."

During the sixteenth century, a wealthy family in South Bohemia (modern-day Czech Republic) dug 460 fishponds in the Trebon Basin region. These fishponds for carp are such a well-respected treasure that the United Nations Educational, Scientific and Cultural Organization declared these ponds a world heritage site. That is indeed high praise for both the carp and the historic importance of those ponds.

These fishponds still produce Christmas carp to this very day. It's a five-year process to raise the carp to the market size of four to five pounds and a length of one and a half feet. In these managed fish farms, the carp eat algae, plankton and some grain. Rye, wheat and triticale are the principal grains fed to larger fish. Those same grains are milled for the younger carp.

To provide the perfect taste, the fish spend their final few months in historic stone-lined tanks closer to the city. That water is free of algae, and it's this more pristine water that improves the flavor and separates Europe's revered carp from America's bottom-feeding, muddy-tasting carp.

For nearly five hundred years, this same farming process and selective fish breeding programs have provided Czechs and Bohemians alike with one of the most sought-after Christmas foods.

## We Want Carp, Too

Europeans craved carp. Upon their arrival in America, immigrants and the well-to-do alike could not believe that carp could not be found in restaurants and/or meat markets. That when newcomers began petitioning the federal government.

Dr. Spencer Baird of the Smithsonian Institution became head of the newly formed United States Commission of Fish and Fisheries in 1876. By 1880, the commission he led was receiving upward of two thousand letters a year clamoring that Baird and his team import carp into America. These requests for carp came at a time when America had no limits. "Carpe diem" was the motto as "everyone seized the day."

Timber was being clear-cut, and fish were netted at will. These two unlimited harvest methods of natural resources combined to devastate native fish populations. Once clear-cutting logging methods ripped the forest floors bare, silt flowed into the rivers and lakes. This silt and mud-covered gravel spawned beds for suckers and walleyes. The muddied water hid food from sight-feeding fish such as the bass. These and other species floundered.

Baird and his team at the U.S. Commission of Fish and Fisheries heard the pleas for carp and jumped to action. To test the waters, Baird imported 345 common, mirror and leather carp in 1877 and 1878 and placed them in ponds near Baltimore and Washington, D.C. Soon the Commission of Fish and Fisheries produced 6,000 carp fingerlings by 1880, and those young carp would be shipped to 273 applicants in twenty-four states. Wisconsin became one of those destinations.

In 1880, about seventy-five common carp, native to Asia, were obtained by the Nevin Hatchery in Fitchburg, Wisconsin. The Wisconsin Fisheries Commission placed as many as thirty-five thousand carp in state waters from 1890 to about 1895 when the program was discontinued. As a result, carp are present in at least sixty of Wisconsin's seventy-two counties.

## PUBLIC OPINION TURNED

The introduction of carp was successful beyond anyone's best projections. The fish flourished in North America's waters. Restaurants and markets began selling carp to demanding customers. Some of New York City's most expensive restaurants were serving "Carp in Rhine Wine Sauce" at prices far higher than those for halibut or kingfish.

However, carp became so plentiful that it not only became the fish of the rich but the "have-not" immigrants, too. America's high rollers soon began eating fish not easily accessible to America's ruffian newcomers. The carp soon became known as a poor man's fish.

The other matter that turned the tide on carp's popularity was taste. In Europe, farm-raised carp were raised like Holsteins and Angus cattle with genetic lines contributing to the best-tasting fish. In America, most fish were being pulled from muddied waters with no genetic selection or grain feeding programs.

"These fish taste like mud!" could often be heard from those eating carp in America. Carp also reproduce at incredible rates and crowd out other native fish. Females can lay up to two million eggs when spawning in spring. As plentiful numbers and poor taste converged, price for carp tumbled. Carp sold for one dollar per pound in the 1890s, and by the 1900s the price had fallen to three to four cents per pound.

## NOW CONSIDERED INVADERS

These days, the common carp is considered one of the most damaging invasive species in America due to its wide distribution and severe impacts in shallow lakes and wetlands. Because these fish are bottom feeders, the carps' feeding patterns dislodge shallow-rooted plants, which results in muddied waters.

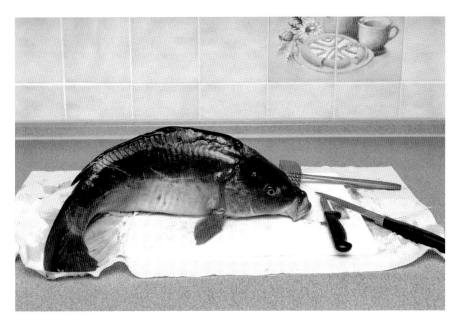

In many homes throughout old Bohemia, the Czech Republic and Germany, carp can still be found on kitchen counters on Christmas Eve or Christmas morning. *istock.*

This in turn releases phosphorus, causing more algae blooms. These carp-induced water-quality issues inhibit aquatic plant species' growth. It's these plants that are needed by native waterfowl and fish. The entire North American ecosystem went catawampus.

After environmental-minded people realized carp were causing these issues, well-orchestrated harvest programs took root. From 1934 to 1974, crews from the Wisconsin Department of Natural Resources routinely harvested carp. These days, there are about ten companies that bid for "rough fish contracts." The high bidder is awarded the right to harvest a lake and pays the state for a permit. Most contract fishing is done in fifteen to twenty-five lakes in southern Wisconsin. Just how much carp has been caught?

From the Koshkonong Lake system alone, which includes the Rock River near Fort Atkinson, over one hundred million pounds of carp have been taken. Most of this fish goes to processing centers in Iowa, New York and Canada. These processed carp then make their way to dinner tables.

It's unlikely that the carp will ever regain its feature-entrée luster in America. However, the fish is here to stay and thrives in Wisconsin waters.

As a child, Julia (Burich) Pritzl ate carp prepared by her Bohemian mother, Anna. As an adult, Julia also prepared carp for her family, but only if the fish was caught in spring, as the cold winter waters dulled the muddy flavor, making it taste far closer to its European relatives.

As for carp in its more native swimming holes, it remains a popular fish to catch and eat throughout Europe and Asia to this very day. And if you spend Christmas in the Czech Republic or southern Germany or celebrate the Chinese New Year in China, carp just may be the only meat source on the menu for these most important of celebrations.

# 27

# It's Time to Speak English

On August 4, 1905, a great standing-room-only celebration was held at Reedsville's St. Mary's Church. Native-born Václav Kubale would soon be ordained a priest. Father Cipin gave a sermon in the community's native tongue, Czech, and Father Kraemer delivered a sermon in English. It took fifty years for English to make its way inside that church.

Times were starting to slowly change, as English was permeating into the area's linguistics. However, the parish faithful invited to the event still received handwritten invitations in the Czech language that the locals simply called Bohemian. Wencel Satorie, his wife and daughter received one such summons. The envelope read:

*Pan Václav Satorie*
*Manzilka a dcera*

The inside invitation read:

*Velp. Václav Karel Kubále*
*Timto vas uctive zve*
*Ku svi prvni msi svate,*
*Ktersou slouziti bude*
*Ve ctvstek 4. srpna o 10. Kodine rano*
*V Chramu Pane*
*Nancbevzeti Panny Marie,*
*V Reedsville, Wis.*

In 1905, the Czech language prevailed in the Reedsville area. This invitation to Father Václav Kubale's first mass was sent to Václav "Wencel" Satorie and his family. *Author's collection.*

The envelope's English translation:

*Mr. Wencel Satorie*
*Wife and daughter*

The invitation's English translation:

*Father Wencel Charles Kubale*
*This is your invitation*
*To the first Mass*
*That will take place*
*On Thursday, August 4, at 10 o'clock in the morning*
*In the Catholic Church of the Lord*
*The Assumption of the Blessed Virgin Mary*
*In Reedsville, Wis.*

St. Mary's was founded originally as a mission church of St. Anne's in Francis Creek. Until that time, a mix of Czech and Latin was spoken during the formal mass, while Bohemian carried the conversation after the church service. In the village streets and farm fields, a mix of Bohemian and German reverberated, as the community had Lutheran and Methodist congregations with German heritages, too.

Those church services rang out in thunderous German as pastors and ministers could be heard saying, "Der Name des Vaters, des Sohnes und des Heiligen Geistes. Amen."

By mid-1918, with the Americans sending their sons back to the European continent that they fled a generation ago, German church services began switching to "In the name of the Father, the Son and the Holy Spirit. Amen."

Other language traditions also started to quickly fade.

## It's Time to Be an American

Nationwide, Germans were a significant immigrant class. They also composed a significant portion of the citizenship. Overall, 9 percent of all those living in America in 1910 still listed Germany as either birth place or as their cultural heritage. In midwestern communities, Germans often made up one-third or even greater portions of the populace.

Germans were industrious farmers and craftsmen. Like other ethnic groups, they were extremely proud of their heritage. That being the case, German Americans spoke to one another in High or Low German in churches and taverns, they read German-language books and those living in this area would even read the local German-language newspaper, the *Manitowoc Pilot*. Since Germany's Bavaria province and Bohemia were neighboring regions in the old country, Czechs and Germans easily understood one another.

However, native-born Americans called Yankees in the day had grown tired of these foreign tongues being spoken on the village streets. To have a prosperous country, everyone must speak the same language.

That's when Wisconsin governor W.D. Hoard and the Republican legislature took action. Just one year after Hoard became governor, Wisconsin's legislature passed the Bennett Law in 1889, and Governor Hoard signed it into law. That law required the use of English to teach major school subjects in all public and private schools. The public part was easy—the private part was not. Wisconsin's immigrant class rebelled at the law's passage.

The Bennett Law was bitterly resented by Wisconsin's German communities. In fact, there was so much disdain for the law that state's Lutheran Missouri Synod and Wisconsin Synod denounced the law. German Catholic priests joined the cause, with Oshkosh's Father Johann Reindl referring to it as "Ungerecht und ein Schlag auf das deutsche Volk!" W.D. Hoard and his Republican allies knew they had set off a powder keg. Father Reindl's statement called the Bennett Law "unjust and a blow at the German people."

The Catholic Archdiocese of Milwaukee, led by Archbishop Fredrick Katzer, became so offended by the Bennett Law they led a groundswell that nominated George Peck as Wisconsin's Democratic nominee for governor. This took place in an era when Wisconsin's Republicans held

Governor Hoard spoke in favor of English being the official language to teach Wisconsin's schoolchildren. Ahead of his time, the Bennet Law would cost Hoard the next election. *Hoard's Dairyman.*

the late President Abraham Lincoln as their party's ideal politician. What's more, Ripon, Wisconsin, was the birthplace of the Republican Party. The Republicans dominated the political landscape.

Despite the growing lovefest between German farmers and their new vocation of dairy farming—championed by W.D. Hoard—the deeply offended Germans carried the day and voted Hoard out of office in 1890 in a 52–43 percent landside. This made Peck the first Democrat to serve as governor since 1855—and the last to serve until Albert Schmedeman in 1932. That same election, voters flipped the state assembly and senate to Democratic control in 1891.

The Democrats got right to work and repealed the Bennett Law. That took place as soon as the legislature was seated in 1891. And tones of both High and Low German dialects rang out once again in classrooms across the Badger State.

The election defeat of 1890 was so devastating that the Republicans did not dare bring up the issue for another two decades. Hoard would never again run for office despite a number of recruitment efforts. Hoard turned all his attention to growing Wisconsin's dairy industry. The Germans had spoken!

# THE GREAT WAR CHANGED EVERYTHING

World War I broke out in in July 1914. America wanted nothing to do with the raging battle. It was an Old World matter. Americans didn't want to send their boys to Europe, as most of them had fled that continent a generation or two earlier.

The wily British knew they might need the Americans to win the war. At least they would need the goods from American factories to fight the entrenchments and dug-in troops on Europe's mainland. Winning the war is one thing; winning minds is another.

On August 5, 1914, a telegram arrived at England's port of Dover—just one day after Britain declared war on Germany. Sent in code, the message was relayed to an officer named Superintendent Bourdeaux. He, along with his unknowing crew on HMS *Alert*, undertook one of the first strategic acts of information warfare in the modern era.

Bourdeaux and his crew dredged up all five German overseas communication cables in the English Channel and severed each one of them. The Germans could no longer communicate freely to Vigo, Tenerife, the Azores and, most importantly, the United States of America. All correspondence had to go through the world's remaining transatlantic telegraph cables, owned by the British.

After that, Great Britain exploited its communication dominance in the international telegraph infrastructure. It deployed nearly six hundred people as censors situated in over one hundred stations around the globe. Together, these code busters and propagandists censored or rewrote over eighty million messages during the Great War—and really picked up the pace after busting the German secret code.

The British would become so successful winning over the minds of the Americans that German Americans would quickly give up speaking the German language on U.S. soil.

# THE TURNING TIDE

With the propaganda machine now at work, the British could exploit stories sent back to America at will. To be fair, the Germans helped the British at times. Sinking the *Lusitania* and killing nearly 1,200 people in 1915 did not help the German cause.

Even so, it was war, and the tide did not turn instantly, as both countries continued to battle for American sympathy. In an effort to master its own propaganda, George Viereck started a German journal, *The Fatherland*. Published out of New York City, *The Fatherland* advocated for "Fair Play for Germany and Austria-Hungary." But it could not stem the plethora of communiqués coming from the British code busters and propagandists.

In 1917, sentiment against German-speaking Americans got worse.

The German government announced it would resume submarine warfare and immediately started sinking American merchant ships it believed were transporting cargo to Great Britain and France. The final straw, however, was the Zimmermann Telegram sent from the German high command to the German ambassador to Mexico. Germany had offered Mexico an alliance if it would go to war with the United States.

Its promise? Mexico would receive Texas, New Mexico and Arizona as the spoils for its pending war effort. This revelation pushed the once apprehensive United States into war against Germany. Britain had won the propaganda war.

## ARE YOU AN AMERICAN?

The American public quickly grew to distrust their first- and second-generation German American neighbors. Those thoughts turned into flames in Manitowoc County's village of St. Nazianz on April 5, 1918. That was almost exactly one year after the United States had declared war on Germany.

The explosion of a gasoline tank was the cause, wrote Father Winfrid Herbst. By the time the fire department arrived from nearby Kiel, a dozen houses and other buildings had been destroyed by the flames. There was great confusion, naturally, and the church bells were ringing nearly all the time, wrote the Salvatorian priest who witnessed the events that day.

One of the reasons the fire spread so quickly was the fact St. Nazianz did not have a fire department to control the flames. What caused that gas tank to explode?

Following America's declaration of war against Germany in 1917, it was not uncommon to hear public expressions of hatred against Germany as a country and against Americans of German descent within this country—particularly against those who still spoke German, wrote the Salvatorians.

The village of St. Nazianz had received a number of anonymous letters protesting the village's public pride in its residents' ancestry throughout

Mary and Frank Pritzl and their eight children routinely spoke German. That all changed when America declared war on Germany in 1917. To prove loyalty to America, those of German heritage gave up their native tongue and began speaking English. *Author's collection.*

1917 and early 1918. The villagers had suspicions how a spark could cause a gas tank explosion in the middle of cold Wisconsin—then ignite a raging fire. Those suspicions were based on those anonymous letters criticizing businesses for what was perceived as "excessive pride in their German heritage" and the fact that visitors to the village heard only German spoken in that community.

While no one was ever arrested or charged for the blaze, the message was sent. And it was received by Wisconsin's German communities.

Businesses that previously bore German names changed to English names, wrote authors of *The Chronicle*, published by the Salvatorian Monastery. Salvatorian publications like the *Manna* magazine, which had previously been published in both German and English, moved to English-only editions.

The St. Nazianz–based Salvatorians discontinued German sermons, devotion and prayers, switching to English. The seminary's German Theatre, which presented plays in German, was officially disbanded ten days later. And lastly, villagers and the Salvatorians began speaking far less German and far more in English. This was not an isolated incident.

## BOHEMIAN FADED TOO

In the Burich household, Bohemian conversations would prevail past World War I. When the family said their final goodbye to Alzbeta (Burich) Kirch in 1923, the tombstone was written in Bohemian.

Just three years later, when thirteen-year-old Cecilia Burich died from polio, that gravestone was etched in English. That also allowed Cecilia's classmates to fully understand its inscription, as English had become the standard language for instruction in all of Wisconsin's public and parochial schools.

By the fall of 1929, the Burich family started speaking English at the dinner table of their own volition when their daughter Mary was being courted by Herbert Kalies from nearby Askeaton. Herb grew up in a largely Irish Catholic community, and he could not speak a lick of Bohemian.

Almost like a mind eraser, Julia Burich lost her ability to recall Bohemian.

As for Cecilia's classmates being instructed solely in English, former Wisconsin governor W.D. Hoard had lived to see another version of the Bennett Law passed by the Wisconsin legislature. English had become the language in which major subjects would be taught in all Wisconsin's schools—both public and parochial.

Of course, it took World War I to convince everyone, "It's time to speak English."

An ornate gravestone expressed Frank Kirch's love for his dear Lizzie, who died far too young at age thirty-eight. In 1923, Frank chose to etch the gravestone in the Czech language. *Author's collection.*

The gravestone for Cecilia Burich set in 1926 was among the very first chiseled in English. Just three years earlier, Cecilia's aunt Elizabeth died and her marker was written in Czech. *Author's collection.*

# 28

# An Education Can Set You Free

**M**a read the newspaper out loud every evening to Pa after we milked the cows," said Julia. "The girls would sit around the kerosene lantern and listen along," she went on. "As Ma read, Pa would puff away on his pipe as he absorbed the latest news."

Curious why a grown man could not simply read the newspaper to himself, Julia's school-aged grandson listening to this account asked the obvious question, "Why did your mom read the newspaper to your dad? Did he have bad eyesight?" asked the inquisitive youngster, tossing out two questions in one breath.

"He only went to school through the second grade," she quipped back. "He didn't know how to read."

A multitude of questions ensued.

## One of Many Illiterates

John Burich wasn't the only grown man in the neighborhood who couldn't read or spell. Sons were the main labor supply for immigrant farmers. Short on labor, his parents, Albert and Josephine, made about the only choice they could back in those days to get the work done: they pulled John out of school after the second grade.

Young John became a farmhand just like his brother Frank, who was four years his elder. John's sisters Anna and Elizabeth were allowed to continue their education, as girls weren't the first source of labor on most farms. Far younger than the entire Burich clan, Thomas—the baby of the family—attended school through the eighth grade because the family could get by with available labor during the school day.

Julia's mother, Anna, was John's classmate. She continued on with her education after John didn't return for third grade. When Anna and John married in 1906, Anna instantly became the farm's bookkeeper. In addition to being the only woman in the family, she was the only one who could read and write both English and Bohemian—not even Anna's father, Wencel, or her father-in-law, Albert, could handle the dual language functions, as English was becoming the language of business.

This inability to read and write is the reason you'll hear the phrase, "Make your mark," when watching older films. That's because some folks couldn't write their names. They literally made an X or some other mark to sign a legal document.

## GRADE SCHOOL BECAME A STANDARD

By the time Julia reached her school days in the 1920s, many of the area's farm families and village-goers had their children attend elementary school and received an eighth-grade education. Julia and her four sisters were among those children.

However, there was no busing. Kids literally hoofed it on foot to school. In rural communities, one-room classrooms dotted the landscape. Meanwhile, Julia walked about two-plus miles to Reedsville's St. Mary's Catholic School.

Since walking was the norm, attendance was far from perfect. That's documented by Julia's fifth- and sixth-grade report cards.

5th Grade, 1st semester, 1st period—Half days present: 54 and half days absent: 4

5th Grade, 1st semester, 2nd period—Half days present: 70 and half days absent: 0

5th Grade, 1st semester, 3rd period—Half days present: 58; half days absent: 18; Times tardy: 2

For immigrant children, an education was a pathway to a better life than their parents'. Shown in this 1920s image are children attending St. Mary's School in Reedsville. *Author's collection.*

6$^{th}$ Grade, 1$^{st}$ semester, 1$^{st}$ period—Half days present: 68 and half days absent: 0

6$^{th}$ Grade, 1$^{st}$ semester, 2$^{nd}$ period—Half days present: 56; half days absent: 6; Times tardy: 1

6$^{th}$ Grade, 1$^{st}$ semester, 3$^{rd}$ period—Half days present: 38; half days absent: 22; Times tardy: 1

In just two years, Julia was absent sixty days—that was just the first semester in fall and early winter. What was the cause?

Most rural farm kids had to help haul in the fall crops. Since those crops had a direct correlation to the family's very survival, the fall harvest trumped going to school.

Julia didn't get a pass from that reality, as her father, John, didn't have any sons. The girls were expected to help with the harvest. On occasion, if there was bad weather—think a blizzard—children were not going to make a four-plus-mile round trip to school.

## School Report

Department of Education
Catholic Diocese of Green Bay

### Elementary Department

PERIODIC, SEMESTRAL, AND ANNUAL REPORT

OF *Julia Burich*

AGE *10* GRADE *VI*

FOR THE SCHOOL YEAR BEGINNING *1929* ENDING *1930*

*Sister M. Matthias* TEACHER

PASTOR *R. Kaliwe*

The parent or guardian is earnestly requested to examine this report, page by page, and to acknowledge its receipt by signing below. Please return this report at once.

SIGNATURE OF PARENT OR GUARDIAN

**First Semester**

1st Period *Mrs. John A. Burich*
2nd Period *Mrs. John A. Burich*
3rd Period *Mrs. John A. Burich*

**Second Semester**

1st Period *Mrs. John A. Burich*
2nd Period *Mrs. John A. Burich*
3rd Period

Form C—3-7-28

**STANDARD AND METHOD OF GRADING**

A  100-95  Exceptionally good work.
B  94-91—Very good.
C  90-85—Good.
D  84-75—Passing.
E  74-71—Failure, but re-examination granted.
F  70 or less—Failure.
G  Absent from examination.
H  Incomplete.

A general average of less than 70 in any branch, and a grand average of less than 75, will not be honored by promotion.
All pupils will take examination at end of each period.
All eighth grade pupils must take the final examination for promotion to High School.
The teacher's estimate will be based on the pupil's daily work, written tests, and the sincere efforts and thoroughness the pupil shows in doing the work assigned.
Enter June examinations in percentages. (•)

| Attendance Deportment Standing | 1st SEMESTER | | | 2nd SEMESTER | | |
|---|---|---|---|---|---|---|
| | 1st Period | 2nd Period | 3rd Period | 1st Period | 2nd Period | 3rd (•) Period |
| Religion | C | C | 88 | B | B | 87 |
| English | C | C | 85 | A | A | 95 |
| Reading | B | B | 91 | A | A | 95 |
| Spelling | B | a | 94 | A | A | 96 |
| History | D | C | 81 | C | C | 81 |
| Civics | | | | | | |
| Arithmetic | C | C | 85 | C | B | 88 |
| Geography | C | D | 75 | C | C | |
| Hygiene | | | | | | |
| Agriculture | | | | | | |
| Science | | | | | | |
| Penmanship | C | a | 90 | B | A | 95 |
| Drawing | | | | | | |
| Music | | | | | | |
| Domestic Science | | | | | | |
| Manual Training | | | | | | |
| Physical Training | | | | | | |
| Effort | B | B | 95 | A | A | 95 |
| Conduct | B | B | 95 | A | A | 90 |
| ½ Days Present | 68 | 56 | 38 | 54 | 48 | 56 |
| ½ Days Absent | — | 6 | 22 | 2 | 6 | — |
| Times Tardy | — | 1 | 1 | — | — | — |

As a sixth-grade student, Julia Burich racked up thirty-six days in which she missed a half day of school. As a result, her grades suffered. This was the case for a number of the area's farm children. *Author's collection.*

## NO SUCH THING AS GRADE INFLATION

Julia's school records also show that the teachers were tough. To simply receive an A was a mighty challenge. The grading scale:

Grade A—100 to 95 "Exceptionally good work"
Grade B—94 to 91 "Very Good"
Grade C—90 to 85 "Good"
Grade D—84 to 75 "Passing"
Grade E—74 to 71 "Failure but reexamination granted"
Grade F—70 or less "Failure"

## School Report

Department of Education
Catholic Diocese of Green Bay

### Elementary Department

PERIODIC, SEMESTRAL, AND ANNUAL REPORT

OF *Burich Julia*

AGE *9 yrs.* GRADE *5*

FOR THE SCHOOL YEAR BEGINNING *6-25* ENDING *6-29*

*Sister M. Louise* TEACHER

PASTOR _____

The parent or guardian is earnestly requested to examine this report, page by page, and to acknowledge its receipt by signing below. Please return this report at once.

**SIGNATURE OF PARENT OR GUARDIAN**

First Semester
1st Period *Mrs. John A. Burich*
2nd Period *Mrs. John A. Burich*
3rd Period *Mrs. John A. Burich*

Second Semester
1st Period *Mrs. John A. Burich*
2nd Period _____
3rd Period _____

Form C—3-7-28

**STANDARD AND METHOD OF GRADING**

A 100–95 Exceptionally good work.
B 94–91—Very good.
C 90–85—Good.
D 84–75—Passing.
E 74–71—Failure, but re-examination granted.
F 70 or less—Failure.
G Absent from examination.
H Incomplete.
A general average of less than 70 in any branch, and a grand average of less than 75, will not be honored by promotion.
All pupils will take examination at end of each period.
All eighth grade pupils must take the final examination for promotion to High School.
The teacher's estimate will be based on the pupil's daily work, written tests, and the sincere efforts and thoroughness the pupil shows in doing the work assigned.
Enter June examinations in percentages. (*)

| Attendance Department Standing | 1st SEMESTER | | | 2nd SEMESTER | | |
|---|---|---|---|---|---|---|
| | 1st Period | 2nd Period | 3rd Period | 1st Period | 2nd Period | 3rd Period |
| Religion | C | B | B | A | A | A |
| English | B | B | B | B | C | B |
| Reading | A | A | A | A | A | A |
| Spelling | A | A | A | A | A | A |
| History | C | C | C | — | — | A |
| Civics | | | | | | |
| Arithmetic | C | B | C | B | B | B |
| Geography | C | C | C | C | C | B |
| Hygiene | | | | | | |
| Agriculture | | | | | | |
| Science | | | | | | |
| Penmanship | B | B | B | B | B | B |
| Drawing | | | | | | |
| Music | | | | | | |
| Domestic Science | | | | | | |
| Manual Training | | | | | | |
| Physical Training | | | | | | |
| Effort | B | B | B | A | A | A |
| Conduct | A | A | A | A | A | A |
| ½ Days Present | 54 | 70 | 58 | 54 | 60 | 68 |
| ½ Days Absent | 4 | | 8 | 6 | | 2 |
| Times Tardy | | | 2 | | | |

This 1928–29 school report for Julia Burich displays the impeccable penmanship from that era. *Author's collection.*

When it came to earning a promotion to the next grade, "A general average of less than 70 in any branch, and a grand average of less than 75 will not be honored by promotion." That was written in distinct text in the *School Report* published by the Department of Education, Catholic Diocese of Green Bay.

Subject areas graded in those fifth- and sixth-grade years included: religion, English, reading, spelling, history, arithmetic, geography and penmanship. In their own separate areas, teachers also assessed effort and conduct. At the end of each period, six in all, the parent or guardian had to sign the report card.

In every case, the near perfect penmanship read, "Mrs. John A. Burich." Remember, Anna was the only one who could read those report cards the girls were bringing home.

## ON TO HIGH SCHOOL

If Julia could obtain her high school diploma, she would have followed in her three adult sisters' footsteps. And in doing so, the Burich family would become one of only a handful of Reedsville clans who had all their children earn a high school diploma.

While an exciting opportunity, the high school still reflected some mundane realities of the day. Those realities included an outhouse.

"When I attended High School at Reedsville," wrote Julia in her journal, "we had to use an outside toilet for three years. When I got to be a senior, they finally installed toilets in the school basement for the 1935 to 1936 term."

Aside from lavatories, Julia clearly revered the opportunity to earn a high school education—so much so that she carefully wrote out the names of the thirty-six students who enrolled as freshmen in the fall of 1932 at Reedsville High School. If these thirty-six youngsters could cross the finish line, they would graduate in the class of 1936.

Julia then placed this list of thirty-six students in her three-inch-thick family Bible. For decades, it resided in the Old Testament's Book of Psalms—Psalm 118 to be exact.

Psalm 118 is the "Hymn of Thanksgiving to the Savior of Israel." It begins, "Alleluia. Give thanks to the Lord, for he is good, for his mercy endures forever."

After reading the Psalm 118 in its entirety, the "mercy" that Julia had in mind was an education. Psalm 118:19–20 reads, "Open to me the gates of justice; I will enter them and give thanks to the Lord." In just a few generations, her family had gone from leaving everything behind in Europe and crossing the Atlantic to making their way to middle America and becoming educated.

By the time 1936 rolled around, only twenty-four students in Julia's class earned their diplomas. That was a dropout rate of 33 percent. Of those students discontinuing their education from 1932 to 1936, there was an equal split between the boys and girls,

For Julia Burich, earning a high school diploma was a momentous achievement. It ranked so high that she kept the names of all her classmates in the family's Bible on the same page as the family tree. *Author's collection.*

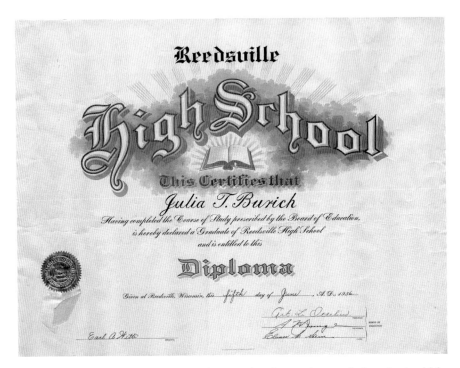

The Reedsville Board of Education clearly wanted students to be proud of graduating high school. Julia Burich's 1936 diploma measures twenty-one inches wide by sixteen inches high. *Author's collection.*

**Class Motto**
"We have crossed the bay, the ocean lies before us"

**Class Colors**
Green and White

**Class Flower**
Tea Rose

**Class Roll**

| | |
|---|---|
| Ruth Bebow | Robert March |
| Irmgard Beil | Grace McCullough |
| Catherine Berger | Ralph Moede |
| Marie Birkholz | Charles Novak |
| Julia Burich | Gordon O'Leary |
| Charles Dvorachek | Marie Phillip |
| Victor Haese | John Pollack |
| Clarence Kocourek | Edward Schroeder |
| Henry Krueger | Elroy Schroeder |
| Helen Kubale | Eileen Sullivan |
| Stanley Kubichka | Mae Belle Utke |
| Carol Maertz | Kenneth Young |

The Senior Class of

Reedsville High School

announces its

Commencement Exercises

Friday evening, June fifth

Nineteen Hundred Thirty-six

Eight o'clock

Memorial Hall

With the class motto, "We have crossed the bay, the ocean lies before us," members of the Reedsville class of 1936 knew earning a high school diploma prepared them for life's challenges. *Author's collection.*

with six in each category. Keep in mind many more students in the same age bracket never entered the threshold of Reedsville High.

For the most part, Reedsville's academic success mirrored America's scholarly movement. In the 1919–20 academic year, just 16.8 percent of all eligible students graduated high school. By 1929–30, 29 percent of eligible high school students were earning degrees. By 1939–40, half of all America's young men and young women graduated high school, according to federal statistics. And of those earning degrees, young men outnumbered the young women.

The Reedsville Board of Education clearly wanted students to be proud of graduating high school. Julia's 1932 diploma measures twenty-one inches wide by sixteen inches high.

It's signed and dated June 5, 1936, by Earl Witte, principal; Art L. Ottehius, president of the board of education; A.H. Junge, treasurer; and Elmer B. Stern, clerk. That diploma was created by the Educational Supply Company of Painesville, Ohio.

Julia's commencement invitation, along with her diploma, was painstakingly preserved. Clearly, for Julia, graduating high school was a major life milestone. The Reedsville class of 1936 that graduated on June 5 of that year in Memorial Hall chose an interesting motto: "We have crossed the bay, the ocean lies before us."

Perhaps these children of first- and second-generation immigrants picked the motto in reference to the dubious sea voyage a generation or two earlier. Perhaps they chose it because they had done what only half their classmates who started out the first grade had done—earned a high school diploma.

# 29

# THE COLLINS MARSH CATTLE DRIVE

The Dirty Thirties—the Burich family never referred to the 1930s as the Great Depression. From a farmer's perspective, a drought was gripping America, and it was inflicting economic woes.

The decade was definitely dirty for those living in America's heartland. It was so dirty that Kansas and Oklahoma were engulfed in what became known as the Dust Bowl. The epic drought caused prairies to dry up and plants to die, and then the winds blew so hard that topsoil eventually filled the air. As the drought gripped middle America, life was changing on the Burich farm, too.

As the 1920s came to a close, John and Anna's daughters started to date and get married. On November 26, 1929, daughter Agnes married George Kubsch. On October 28, 1930, daughter Mary wed Herbert Kalies.

With the good times rolling, John and Anna did the unthinkable for a farm couple of that era: the proud parents gave daughters Agnes and Mary $5,000 each as wedding gifts. The Burich family farm had been prosperous, and John and Anna wanted to share their bounty with their children.

With the first set of newlyweds off to a good start, the grandchildren—more specifically grandsons—soon followed. Agnes and George welcomed two children: Janice and George. Mary and Herbert had four sons prior to 1937: Jack, Ronald, Ken and Herbert Jr. A fifth boy, John, was born one month after the third Burich daughter, Beatrice, married Quiren Sleger on September 14, 1937. In celebration of that marriage, John and Anna also gifted the Slegers $5,000.

However, Anna was concerned that these wedding and early inheritance gifts now should be held off, especially the last one to Beatrice, as she knew money was evaporating with the parched earth of the Dirty Thirties. John insisted upon giving the gift.

Up until this point, John thought he could just push through the economic downturn with his "work like a mule" attitude. However, John was now in his late fifties, and at times, he was struggling to catch his breath.

Outside of this evolving situation, John was happy. He had both men and boys on the farm to help him now. Not only did John have three strapping sons-in-law to assist with projects, but two of those young men had families that dairy farmed for a living as well. On top of that, John now had six grandsons. A steady supply of labor was waiting in the wings.

While he was flush with help, feed inventories were getting low for not only the Burich family farm but also the Kalies and Sleger families. Industrious and innovative John had a plan to combat the drought.

## DESPERATE TIMES. DESPERATE MEASURES.

Where might there be water during an extended drought? The marshes!

There was no state-owned Collins Marsh in the 1930s. Most of the land was held by farmers. John Burich was one such landowner, as were nearby neighbors Frank Kirch, Louis Turensky, William Rusch, A.H. Rusch, William Klann and others.

Where was that land?

When traveling just a few miles south from Reedsville on what became State Route 32, there's a major bend as the highway curves west. In those days, farmers also could drive straight at that curve onto a dead-end road called "Minnesota Junction." That road extended over one and a half miles deep into the modern-day interior of the Collins Marsh.

It's at that location that John Burich owned a forty-acre parcel of land. In the 1930s, it just may have saved his farm and those of his relatives. "In the drought and Depression years, my dad started planting timothy in the Collins Marsh," said Julia. "We made hay there; I helped make hay, too." At that time, Julia was a teenager.

As for the accuracy of the timothy crop? The first-ever aerial images taken by USDA in 1938 show cultivation and a timothy crop planted on that land.

## Potatoes Grew There, Too

"Dad was downright worried that we might starve," said Julia. "So, we planted potatoes in the marsh, too. Boy, did we grow some potato crops. Those crops flourished until the rains returned. Then the potatoes would rot right in the field. There's a reason that farmers grow potatoes on irrigated sand ground. That's because potatoes need good drainage."

"It was so hot in those days," recalled Julia, responding as if she were wiping perspiration from her brow. "We also pastured heifers there."

"I helped with one trip," said Julia's husband, Elmer Pritzl, with a smile as if he just transcended back to his late teenage years.

"Herb Kalies had some heifers, and so did Quiren Sleger," said Elmer, who started dating Julia in 1937.

The Kalies and Sleger families weren't exactly neighbors. Quiren was farming near Kellnersville while Herb was farming near Askeaton—both nearly fourteen miles from the Burich family homestead.

"They literally herded those heifers over to my future father-in-law's farm. We herded them to the marsh the next day," Elmer said. "We would chase the heifers over five miles to the marsh," added Julia. "Boy was that fun!" she exclaimed with an extreme note of sarcasm.

These dairy heifers and beef steers needed feed. With his crops on high ground drying up due to drought, John Burich had a cattle drive to water in the modern-day Collins Marsh. *Author's collection.*

With no brothers, Julia often helped with farm work. On the day of a cattle drive, Julia would wear a pair of her father's more durable pants. *Author's collection.*

## Stood as Sentinels

"Each girl had to stand in the gateway," said Julia. The girls were the four living sisters: Mary, Agnes, Beatrice and Julia. As for standing in the driveway, that was done on horseback.

"Each farm had a gate and we needed to stand in it, so the heifers would keep running," she said.

"You must remember, everything was fenced in those days," she said of the area, reconfirming that farmers grazed their calves, heifers and cows on pasture.

"I don't know how we did it. Man, we didn't have any problems," said Julia. "Watering heifers was pretty easy." And of course, during the Dirty Thirties, water is what everyone was after.

"Pa found a spring down there," she said of his forty-acre parcel in the modern-day Collins Marsh.

"Out came his dynamite. He set off a charge and the water ran. Those heifers had a pond and all the water that they could drink," said Julia, who witnessed the occasion, having ridden her horse to the site the day her father unleashed the explosives.

"It actually became an artesian well and the water ran all the time," recalled Elmer, who later owned the property with his wife, Julia.

"It was good water," she confirmed.

And so, the extended Burich family pastured their heifers on their land in the Collins Marsh throughout the 1930s as a way to survive the Dirty Thirties. It took a cattle drive to deliver the water.

# 30

# SAVE OUR SOIL

While John Burich had developed a coping strategy for the Dirty Thirties, the family farm was struggling. The Burich family wasn't alone, as nearly everyone in the rural countryside was suffering from the same plight.

The Roaring Twenties roared so loud and so strong that no one in America thought it would ever come to an end. However, with history in the rear-view mirror, the decade's roaring economy eventually set the stage for the worst economic tragedy in human history.

By the time the 1920s arrived on the scene, World War I was quickly becoming a distant memory. America's factories glowed with red-hot activity. As manufacturing roared, trains whistled and cars rolled down roads, the era became flush with wealth. People thought a new economic paradigm had settled across America, and they spent money ever more freely.

However, a disturbing pressure cooker had been building across middle America.

## AGRICULTURE LEFT BEHIND

As Americans in cities prospered, their agricultural cousins were quietly slipping into financial despair. That's because U.S. farmers continued producing food at a pace as if they were still feeding war-ravaged Europe. But Europe's economy and the continent's farm fields were being restored. That being the case, its citizens no longer needed America's farm produce.

During the war years and the ensuing 1920s, generous U.S. federal farm policies created a land boom. In the southern plains, farmers plowed up an estimated 5.2 million acres of virgin grasslands. With ample rains from unusually wet years, farmers planted and reaped a wheat harvest like none seen before in human history.

Then the rains stopped. The dust formed. The Great Depression and Dust Bowl rained down on America.

## BLACK DAYS SHOWERED DOWN

America's economic engine seized when its financial sector crashed on three tragic days in late October 1929. The days were dubbed black—black as in a funeral. And it was a funeral, as Americans jumped from buildings, taking their lives due to economic ruin.

Heat waves parched the earth. Dearth and dust storms swept across middle America. When it stopped raining in 1931, a drought began that would last through the 1930s.

While dust storms brewed for three years prior, 1934 became the harbinger of an even more deeply disastrous drought. An estimated 75 percent of the country felt the effects of the dust squalls.

Leaders in Washington, D.C., had been hearing reports of the dreadful drought. The U.S. Department of the Interior created a pilot project to protect public land. And on September 19, 1933, Hugh Hammond Bennett became leader of the newly created Soil Erosion Service. Wisconsin became an epicenter for this soil-saving work.

Raymond Davis, superintendent of the Upper Mississippi Valley station near La Crosse, Wisconsin, was the very first experiment station director to secure the cooperation of nearby farmers to install terraces. "Thus, the nearby Coon Creek was designated project number 1 in November and January 1934," wrote Douglas Helms, a national historian with USDA's Natural Resources Conservation Service.

As these pilot projects took root, even Democratic president Roosevelt remained concerned about spending public money on private land. The 1935 dust storms changed that thought process.

## SAVE OUR SOIL

"A yellow haze appeared over Washington before noon on Wednesday, March 6," wrote Helms. "The Weather Bureau reported that pilots observed thick dust at 8,000 feet elevation above Bolling Field, south of the Capitol." Two weeks later, as Bennett was making his case before a House Committee on Public Lands, Washington, D.C., became engulfed in a dusty haze that nearly blotted out the setting sun.

"Creeping halfway across the Nation in a murky cloud extending 10,000 feet into the sky, the great dust storm of the Southwest and Midwest invaded the East yesterday, bringing grime and discomfort on the first day of spring," reported the *Washington Post* in its March 22, 1935 edition.

"Even as the Administration determined upon a combined drive by seven government agencies to fasten the Midwest's rich farm soil against the destructive dust storms, the swirling particles of earth from Kansas, Oklahoma and Texas sifted into the District and dirtied the windows of Federal Buildings," wrote reporters.

"To a large extent the storm, which traveled at an estimated speed of 35 miles an hour, passed to the north of the Capital, but by late afternoon it was distinctly visible here. A clay-colored veil hung before the Washington Monument, the Lincoln Memorial, the Capitol and the Library of Congress."

On April 14, 1935, Black Sunday settled across parts of the Unites States. While the morning started out as a clear, bright day, the skies turned black from the Dakotas all the way to Texas. Reports indicated it was darker than night. Some churchgoing settlers believed that Armageddon foretold in the Holy Bible's book of Revelation had come to earth.

"More dirt was moved in that one day, in that one storm, than was excavated during the 10 years of construction of the Panama Canal," wrote Beth Dippel for the Sheboygan County Historical Research Center. "This was the event that prompted a Lubbock report to coin the term, 'Dust Bowl.'" Words were no longer needed to tell the story. America's topsoil was blowing away and with it America's future ability to grow food.

Eventually, Bennett's pilot project—the Soil Erosion Service—was transferred from the U.S. Department of the Interior to the U.S. Department of Agriculture. "The agency later changed its name to the Natural Resources Conservation Service (NRCS) and expanded its mission from reducing soil erosion to conserving all natural resources," wrote Taylor.

## DEATH ON THE FARM

It took some time to roll these programs out to all the nation's farms. In fact, it took so long that John Burich died from congestive heart failure.

On February 10, 1939, a somber Mrs. John A. Burich put pen to paper as Harry R. Haese sat across the kitchen table in her home. Haese was the local committeeman for USDA's Agricultural Conservation Program. It was a meeting with few words as Anna had literally buried her husband on February 9—just one day earlier.

Anna would follow through with John's plan and sign the documents even though the papers were filled with the pronoun "he." She also completed the paperwork for her forty acres of the family homestead that her father, Wencel Satorie, sold to her just prior to her marriage. The paperwork for that property had her name on it: Mrs. John A. Burich.

When taking a deeper look at the 1939 form signed by Anna, the Agricultural Conservation Program had two categories: soil depleting and non-depleting. Farmers received land payments placed in non-depleting crops. Anna received seventy-five dollars in her first year, based on the worksheet calculation completed by Haese: twelve points for the Burich homestead and four points for the Satorie homestead.

Haese was making his way through the area, as the 1930s had left many farmers strapped for money. It may be the very reason Haese showed up just one day after John Burich's funeral. With Anna's signature, Haese could get the widow seventy-five dollars.

Corn and wheat were the main USDA soil-depleting crops. Any farm with a corn allotment of eight acres or less is considered a non–corn allotment farm. The corn acreage will be considered general soil-depleting for the purpose of computing a payment. Any acres planted in corn in excess of eight acres will be subject to the regular corn rate of deduction.

The same language applied to wheat. Now grain crops like barley and oats got a pass in comparison to wheat. That pass came only if barley and oats were planted

By 1939, Anna had complete control of the farm's reins. She no longer had a male living blood relative, and her husband, John, had died that February. *Author's collection.*

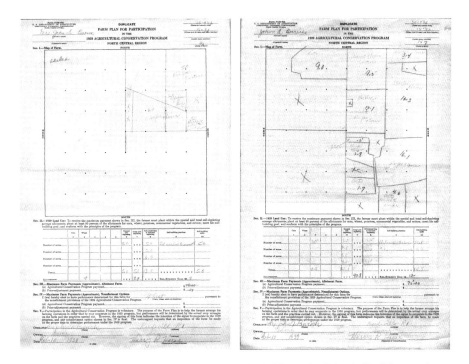

*Left*: By voluntarily entering into an agreement with USDA, Mrs. John A. Burich agreed to abide by practices to conserve and save topsoil. *Author's collection.*

*Right*: When looking at the Agricultural Conservation Program map, an area marked with an X is either a woods or not owned by the farmer. *Author's collection.*

with companion or "cover crop" with alfalfa, white clover, sweet clover, red clover, alsike clover or a variety of grasses.

That's because barley or oats would "cover" or "shelter" the legumes and grasses in the early stages of development from drying out in the midday sun. By the time the barley or oats were ready for harvest, the grasses and legumes could fend for themselves. Since wheat was a fall crop, it didn't work in the system, as oats and barley were planted in spring with the legumes and grasses.

That year, Anna committed to either planting or maintaining: 47.6 acres of alsike clover, 9.5 acres to sweet clover pasture, 7.0 acres to alfalfa pasture, 4.6 acres of oats seeded to alsike clover, 15.1 acres of barley seeded to alsike clover, 10.7 acres of oats and 0.5 acres of potatoes.

In reviewing those historic 1939 documents, some farmers say those forms remain quite similar to those used by NRCS to this very day.

As for the legacy of the Soil Conservation Service, over the past eighty-five years, NRCS has worked with farmers and ranchers to put conservation on more than ninety-seven million acres of agricultural and forest lands nationwide.

"Many conservation practices help improve soil quality—because healthy soils are the foundation for healthy working lands," wrote Taylor. "Furthermore, USDA studies show that soil erosion is reduced by 43 percent on lands that use conservation practices." That conservation movement, along with some desperately needed rains, eventually put an end to the Dust Bowl.

# 31

# WILL YOU RUN MY FARM?

S eventy years.

For seventy years, an envelope postmarked August 18, 1939, rested on Elmer Pritzl's nightstand; that letter was found resting next to his prayer book upon his passing. After reading that precious letter for the first time, there is no doubt the envelope, and the double-sided letter it contained, provided insight into Elmer's most prized earthly possession.

That possession would be his farm and the relationship that came with it upon marrying his bride, Julia Burich.

To read and fully comprehend that letter sends one back to another time, when cultural norms were much different from those of today.

The letter writer was Anna Burich, Elmer's mother-in-law of just over fourteen months. She had addressed the letter to *Mr. Elmer Pritzl, Brillion, Wis.* The newlyweds were living in Brillion right next door to his childhood friend Rudy Seljan—as in Brillion's famed Rudy's Café.

On the bottom of the envelope, Elmer inscribed this short message: "Something to cherish from Mom." Anna, however, was his mother-in-law.

## SHE WANTED A SON OF HER OWN

Let's travel back to immigrant America and its hierarchy of traditions that traced far back to medieval Europe and even to the ancient Egyptians.

A baby boy meant everything to a husband and wife. A boy meant the continuation of the family line. A boy meant hope of brawn and brilliance for the future of the family business.

In old age, a boy provided assurance that someone would care and provide for you. After all, there was no social services such as Social Security or Medicaid.

The first-born boy carried even more privilege than his younger brothers and definitely his sisters. He would inherit the vast majority of the family's wealth, while others would often find their own way in the world around them.

Born on July 6, 1877, Anna Satorie grew up in an immigrant home with no male. Anna's older sister married well before Anna reached adulthood, and Anna lived with her parents, Wencel and Anna, far past the age that a woman would marry in those days. That's because she was caring for her elderly parents and doing the farm work meant for a son.

## Until Death Do Us Part, Father

With her mother's passing in 1905, her father, Wencel, bucked the cultural norms and sold his forty-acre farm to a girl, his dear Anna, for one dollar. She had just turned twenty-six, and all her schoolmates were already married with children of their own.

In exchange, Anna would care for her father until his death. This was written on the deed of the farm transfer. Anna dutifully and lovingly carried out the terms of that contract until Wencel died in 1920.

With that contract, Anna Satorie also became the area's first woman landowner. For her entire life, even after she married John Burich on June 12, 1906, that land stayed in her name; all other Rockland Township parcels were held by men. After her marriage, the plat books changed from "Anna Satorie" to "Mrs. John A. Burich." Same woman, different names. This was before women even earned the constitutional right to vote.

## Plenty of Men, but No Boys

Anna; her husband, John; John's father, Albert; her brother-in-law Louis; and her father, Wencel, all lived together in the family's pioneer house. Anna lost her first-born baby boy, Wencel Burich, just hours after he entered the world on September 15, 1907. Two daughters, Mary and Agnes, followed on December 25, 1909, and May 1, 1911, respectively.

Anna then gave birth to another son, Adolph, on June 18, 1912. He lived five days. This was the last boy she would give birth to and cradle. Next, three more daughters joined the family: Cecilia, born September 27, 1913, Beatrice, born April 14, 1915, and then the youngest, Julia, born October 30, 1918.

Julia had a deep admiration for her father, John. And like her mother, Anna, Julia was the baby of the family. Julia remained at home well after all her sisters married and moved away. When caring for and milking the family's twenty-plus dairy cows, Julia would often wear her father's barn clothes. The father-daughter team also hauled milk to the local cheese factory. Julia had become a hardworking woman, just like her mother.

Elmer entered the scene in 1937. In order to take Julia on her first date, he had to borrow a buddy's car. He then headed to the Burich farm. Upon seeing the massive home, Elmer just drove by the farm and further studied the situation.

"Could that be the right house?" he thought to himself. He pulled in the driveway, and out came Julia, with her parents surveying the situation from the window before coming out to talk to the young man.

Elmer and Julia fell in love. Not yet in their twenties, Julia had a big ask of Elmer. "I want to have my dad walk me down the down the aisle and dance with me on my wedding day." Elmer knew instantly that Julia wanted to get married—and real soon. He proposed and essentially moved up their wedding.

Julia's dreams barely happened in June 1938, as the once vibrant Bohemian father was suffering from congestive heart failure. John mustered enough strength to walk his daughter down the aisle and would dance just one dance.

In the meantime, Julia knew the family was in financial trouble, as the Dirty Thirties eroded the Buriches' net worth. Knowing all that, Julia and her mother mutually agreed that the newlyweds would not receive the $5,000 cash wedding present received by the three eldest daughters. That could wait for a sunnier economic day.

And with nearly two hundred acres, and in quickly failing health, John took preemptive action and worked out an arrangement with his oldest daughter, Mary, and her husband, Herb Kalies, to rent the farm with an option to buy. Following the cultural norms of the day, John handpicked

John Burich would live just long enough to see his youngest daughter, Julia, marry Elmer Pritzl on June 16, 1938. By the end of 1939, the couple would be running the family farm. *Author's collection.*

The Burich family shown shortly after the death of John Burich. *Author's collection.*

Mary and Herb because the couple had already had five sons, John and Anna's grandsons. Those five boys swayed John on that decision.

Within eight months, John died.

Even though Mary and Herb Kalies were running the farm, Elmer was earning a special place in Anna's heart. Like her husband, John, Elmer had a "work like a mule" ethic, and he appeared as honest as the pure driven snow.

Anna made up her mind, "Elmer, will you walk me into church for John's funeral?"

"Yes," Elmer said as he blushed. Elmer walked Anna into St. Mary's on February 9, 1939, with his bride of less than eight months walking next to him.

That day, John A. Burich was laid to rest in the new St. Mary's cemetery. John was only the second person buried there, and the gravesite was so new that no grave marker would be set for months.

## Tough Financial Road

"My dad originally wanted my oldest sister, Mary, to buy the farm, but that fizzled out," recalled Julia. "Mary had five boys, and Pa figured she had enough help. But then they couldn't swing it financially. It got so tough in 1939 that Ma borrowed money from Mary Shimek just to pay the bills. The $1,000 note was at 4 percent interest."

It just so happens that original loan note, with documentation of its payment in full, also was stored away in later years with the letter from Anna to Elmer.

That spring, Julia's sister Agnes and her husband, George, gave it a try. That didn't fare much better. The barns were literally empty heading into the fall. As this situation unfolded, Julia and Elmer expressed interest in running the farm.

"I had saved a lot of money working at the Brillion Foundry," said Elmer. "In 1939, I was earning seventeen cents an hour as a foreman, up from ten cents before my promotion." He had been working at the Brillion Iron Works since graduating high school in 1934 at the age of sixteen. He had been saving up for five years.

Anna must have liked what she saw in Elmer and her daughter Julia. Plus, the young couple had what other family members lacked—money.

"The rest of the money we borrowed from the Calumet County Bank of Brillion," noted Julia, who also explained that she never took her $5,000 wedding present from her folks because they simply didn't have the cash.

"Mary and her husband, Herb, also had other options. His folks had a farm near Askeaton," said Julia. "Then, Mary and Herb bought a cheese factory and went into the cheese making business."

## Elmer's Cherished Letter

*Reedsville, Wis.,*
*August 18, 1939*

*Dear Children,*
*How are you?*

*I am feeling yet good, but I can't sleep well as I was at Beattie's helping thresh Monday. I came home that evening and they were not done yet. Now I heard they were threshing on Holy Day morning. I heard they threshed 1,140 bushels.*

*I want you to come down Sunday after church and decide about the farm. Mr. Sedvina* [attorney] *has not sent me a letter yet, but it's in the paper again* [John's final probate to settle a number of loans on land deed]. *I think we should measure the farm's acreage, along with that new barn, and you would only need to build a house. That barn is big enough for cows, horses, pigs, and everything you need for feed storage.*

*I will sell all my clover seed.*

*Come over Sunday. The rest we will talk over.*

*Best regards.*

*From your Mother.*

*P.S. A. and G.* [Agnes and George] *wants to go to the county fair Sunday in Manitowoc, so come over for early.*

## A Special Place in Her Heart

Anna quickly changed her business plans initially written in pencil on that August day.

By the end of those Sunday afternoon negotiations, Anna, Elmer and Julia had worked out a verbal agreement. The newlyweds would move into the farmhouse and immediately begin running the farm. There would be no need for a land surveyor and a second home.

Anna had choice of two rooms in the upstairs of the farmhouse, and the trio would dine together for the rest of Anna's life—breakfast, lunch and dinner—sixteen more years. As fate would have it, that was exactly the same time frame that Anna cared for her father, Wencel.

During that time, Elmer and Anna's bond became so strong that Elmer always called Anna "Mother." Elmer's wife, Julia, who called her mother "Ma," would quip that Elmer may have loved Anna more than her.

While that's not true, Anna and Elmer gave each other what no one else could provide.

Elmer's mother was killed by a train in 1932. And Anna provided that motherly figure he had been searching for in his life ever since his mother's passing. Coincidentally, Elmer's mother was also named Anna.

In Elmer, Anna finally had a son. In Anna, Elmer had a mother.

No "in-law" was needed to define the relationship. The family farm once again had a future.

That future now lay in the hands of Elmer and Julia.

# Bibliography

Allen, Terese. *Hometown Flavor: A Cook's Tour of Wisconsin's Butcher Shops, Bakeries, Cheese Factories, and Other Specialty Markets*. Madison, WI: Prairie Oak Press, 1998.

Ambrose, Stephen E. *Nothing Like It in the World: The Men Who Built the Transcontinental Railroad, 1863–1869*. New York: Simon & Schuster, 2000.

Apple, R.W. "The Meat That Made Sheboygan Famous." *New York Times*, June 5, 2002.

Austin, H. Russell. *The Wisconsin Story: The Building of a Vanguard State*. Milwaukee, WI: North American Press, 1948.

Brady, Frank, *Crandon: Its Industries and Resources*. Crandon, WI: Brady & Son, Printers, 1906.

Bray, Robert. "History of Meat Science." https://meatscience.org/about-amsa/history-mission/history-of-meat-science.

Brown, Candace. "Flushing's Second REO, 1927 REO Speed Wagon with Boyer Body." *Vintage Fire Truck & Equipment*, May–June 2017, 60–67.

Buffler, Rob, and Tom Dickson. *Fishing for Buffalo: A Guide to the Pursuit, Lore, and Cuisine of Buffalo, Carp, Mooneye, Gar, and Other "Rough" Fish*. Minneapolis, MN: Culpepper Press, 1990.

Bureau of Land Management. "Land Description Diagram." https://www.blm.gov/or/pubroom/files/land-descript-diag.pdf, 2020.

Busse, Fire Chief Brad. "Fire Department History." Village of Reedsville. https://www.reedsville.org/departments/fire-department.

Cairns, C.A., Passenger Traffic Manager. *Chicago and Northwestern Line Time*, Table 36, page 30; Table 42, page 31, March 1928.

Cavanaugh, William F. "How Milwaukee County Keeps Its Roads Open in Winter." *Concrete Highway Magazine*, March 1920, 51–53.

Centers for Disease Control and Prevention. "FastStats—Life Expectancy." https://www.cdc.gov/nchs/fastats/life-expectancy.htm.

Corera, Gordon. "How Britain Pioneered Cable-Cutting in World War One." *BBC News*, December 15, 2017. https://www.bbc.com/news/world-europe-42367551.

Davidson, Peter. "Presence of the Past, Section 4." North Gower, Ontario. http://northgower.tripod.com/buildings/moving.htm.

Dippel, Beth. "Effects of Dust Bowl Felt in Wisconsin." *Wisconsin State Farmer*, October 19, 2018.

Draeger, Jim, and Mark Speltz. *Bottoms Up: A Toast to Wisconsin's Historic Bars & Breweries*. Madison: Wisconsin Historical Society Press, 2012.

DuPont Corporation. *Farming with Dynamite: A Few Hints to Farmers*. Baltimore, MD: Lord Baltimore Press, 1910.

Dushek, Camille, Mrs. George Pribyl, Clarence Spevancheck and Dan Juchniewich. *Bohemians Prominent in Manitowoc County History*. Occupational Monograph 38, 1979 Series, 1–8, Manitowoc County Historical Society, 1979.

Editors, Special to *Press Gazette*. "Rev. Frank Kolar Observes Golden Jubilee on Tuesday." *Green Bay Press Gazette*, April 22, 1939.

Ehlert, Edward. *The Development of the Dairy Industry in Manitowoc County*. Occupational Monograph 11, 1970 Series, 1–8, Manitowoc County Historical Society, 1970.

———. *From Forest to Crop Land*. Occupational Monograph 7, 1969 Series, 1–8, Manitowoc County Historical Society, 1969.

Falge, Dr. Louis. *History of Manitowoc County Wisconsin*. Vol. 2. Chicago: Goodspeed Historical Association, 1912.

Fourshee, Paul. "The Blueprint, History of Nails." *The Blueprint* 1, no. 2 (April 1990). https://www.fourshee.com/history_of_nails.htm.

Geiger, Corey A. "Wisconsin Is Experiencing a Dairy Renaissance." *Hoard's Dairyman*, November 2014.

Green Bay Packers. "Humble Beginnings 1919–1929." https://www.packers.com/legacy-documentary/humble-beginnings-packers-legacy-1919-1929.

Hátle, Miroslav. "Trebon Basin." United Nations Educational, Scientific and Cultural Organization, May 2012. http://www.unesco.org.

Helms, Douglas. "Hugh Hammond Bennett and the Creation of the Soil Conservation Service, September 19, 1933–April 27, 1935." *Historical Insights*, March 2010.

Herman, Syd. "Sparks from the Campfire." *Lakeshore Chronicle*, May 11, 1991.

Histories of the National Mall. "Black Blizzard Blankets the National Mall." http://mallhistory.org/items/show/167.

History.com editors. "Homestead Act." https://www.history.com/topics/american-civil-war/homestead-act.

Hoever, Reverend Hugo. *Lives of the Saints*. New York: Catholic Book Publishing, 1955.

Hout, Michael, and Alexander Janus. "Educational Mobility in America: 1930s–2000s." Working paper, University of California–Berkeley, November 8, 2008. Survey Research Center, Berkeley, CA.

Janda, Robert. *Entertainment Tonight*. Occupational Monograph 28, 1976 Series, 1–8, Manitowoc County Historical Society, 1976.

Johnson, Carol. *Lighting the Landscape*. Hammond, WI: St. Croix Electric Cooperative Office, 2012.

Kanetzke, Howard. "Lime, One of Wisconsin's Oldest Industries." *Wisconsin Trails*, Autumn 1969.

Kanetzke, Howard, and Reinhart Wessing. *Limestone, An Important and Valuable Manitowoc County Resource*. Occupational Monograph 27, 1975 Series, 1–8, Manitowoc County Historical Society, 1975.

Kennedy, Heide. "Carp for Cash." *Lake Tides* 36, no. 1 (Winter 2011): 1–4.

Kirch, Alzbeta. Obituary, *Manitowoc Pilot*, December 6, 1923.

Kubale, Bernard. *The Place to Meet Your Friends*. N.p.: Elabuk Press, 2017.

Lacy, Jim. "UW-Madison to Digitally Archive Historic 1937–1941 Aerial Photographs." State Cartographers Office, https://www.sco.wisc.edu.

Ladwig, Tim, and John Neale. *Good King Wenceslas*. Cambridge, UK: Eerdmans Books for Young Readers, 2005.

Lau, Diane. *History of Collins, Wisconsin*. Self-published, 1996.

Law, Chairman James. *State Highway Commission of Wisconsin 1835–1945*. Madison, WI: self-published, 1947.

Long, Father Tom. *Parish Directory Jubilee Year 2000*. Brillion, WI, 2000.

Mack, Henrietta, Connie Koerth and Nancy Ott. *History of the Town of Maple Grove, Manitowoc County, Wisconsin*. Reedsville, WI: self-published, 2000.

Maraniss, David. *When Pride Still Mattered: A Life of Vince Lombardi*. New York: Simon & Schuster, 2000.

Meany, Winifred. "Reedsville News." *Herald Times Reporter*, December 30, 1926.

Meyer, Amy. "Tuberculosis Left Its Mark on Manitowoc." *Herald Times Reporter*, April 16, 2016.

Moore, Sam. "The Delco-Light Plant—Farm Life." *Farm Collector*, January 2013. https://www.farmcollector.com.

Muldoon, Bishop Peter J. *The National Catholic War Council Bulletin* 1, no. 5 (November 1919).

National Parks Service. "History of Common Carp in North America." https://www.nps.gov/miss/learn/nature/carphist.htm.

Nelson, Rob. "The Farm Light Plant." The Farm Light Plant—The Official Delco-Light Plant Collectors Site. http://delcolight.com/20.html.

Neuser, Father John. *St. Mary's Parish Directory*. St. Mary's Parish, Reedsville, WI, 1972.

Orr, David. *The Road Not Taken*. New York: Penguin Press, 2013.

Oshinsky, David. *Polio: An American Story*. New York: Oxford University Press, 2005.

Osman, Loren H. *W.D. Hoard: A Man for His Time*. Fort Atkinson, WI: W.D. Hoard & Sons Company, 1985.

Pauli, Herta E. *Alfred Nobel: Dynamite King—Architect of Peace*. New York: L.B. Fischer Publishing Corporation, 1942.

Prague Tours–Private Guided Tours. "Saint Wenceslas (Václav): The Czech Nation's Patron Saint." https://www.private-prague-guide.com/article/saint-wenceslas-vaclav-the-czech-nations-patron-saint/.

Prigge, Ed. "Take a Trip Through Manitowoc County's Ghost Towns." *Herald Times Reporter*, October 12, 2014.

Public Broadcasting Service. "Nitroglycerin. An American Experience." https://www.pbs.org/wgbh/americanexperience/features/tcrr-nitroglycerin/.

Rappel, Joseph J. *A Story of a Century: Manitowoc County During Wisconsin's First Hundred Years, 1848–1948*. Manitowoc, WI: Manitowoc County Centennial Committee, 1948.

Roberts, Gary L. *Doc Holliday: The Life and the Legend*. Hoboken, NJ: John Wiley & Sons, 2006.

Rockland, Town of, Manitowoc County, Wisconsin. *Land Use Planning Document*, March 1980.

Roll, David L. *George Marshall: Defender of the Republic*. New York: Penguin Random House, 2013.

Roznik, Sharon. "Moonshine in the Holyland." *FDL Reporter*, December 26, 2015. www.fdlreporter.com/story.

Schmidt, Steve. "House Moving in the Early 1900s." shiawasseehistory.com.

Selner, Raymond. *The Czech Catholic Parishes in Northeast Wisconsin as Chronicled by Father Adalbert "Vojtech" Cipin*. Denmark, WI: self-published, 2010.

Simon, Kenneth A., and Vance W. Grant. *Digest of Educational Statistics, Bulletin Number 4. Table 1, 1964 Edition*. Washington, D.C.: U.S. Department of Health, Education, and Welfare, Government Printing Office, 1965.

Society of the Divine Savior Salvatorians. "St. Nazianz Fire." www.salvatorians.com.

Stanchfield, D.L. *About Forest County Wisconsin, The Heart of the Great Hardwood Country*. Crandon, WI: D.L. Stanchfield Printer, 1914.

Swift, Louis Franklin, and Arthur Van Vlissingen. *The Yankee of the Yards: The Biography of Gustavus Franklin Swift*. New York: A.W. Shaw Company, 1927.

Taylor, Ciji. "PBS Film Explores History of Dust Bowl and Founding of USDA Agency." USDA. www.usda.gov.

Trimble, Megan. "These Countries Drink the Most Beer." *U.S. News & World Report*, September 30, 2017. https://www.usnews.com.

U.S. Census Bureau. "Historical Marital Status Tables." www.census.gov/data/tables/time-series/demo/families/marital.html.

Wenzel, Beth, Kris Bastian, Darcy Zander-Feinauer, Lisa Sprangers and Joey Diener. *Brillion Wisconsin, 1885–2010*. Brillion, WI: Zander Press, Brillion, 2017.

Werblow, Steve. "Christmas Carp". *The Furrow* (Moline, IL), January 9, 2019. https://www.johndeerefurrow.com/2018/12/17/christmas-carp.

Wilbur, Margaret Hobbs. *Remembering Elmyra Hobbs*. Crandon, WI: self-published, 2013.

Winterbotham, J.M., Secretary. *Railroad Commission, State of Wisconsin, Volume X, 23*. August 1912 to 13 November 1912, page 596. Democrat Printing Company, State Printer, 1913.

Wüstenbecker, Katja. "German-Americans during World War I." Immigrant Entrepreneurship. German Historical Institute. https://www.immigrantentrepreneurship.org/entries/german-americans-during-world-war-i/.

Zarnoth, Dorothy, ed. *History of Reedsville to 1976*. Brillion, WI: Zander Press, 1976.